TEACHING THE LANGUAGE OF TIME

Marilyn M. Toomey
artist
Susan Christy-Pallo

CIRCUIT PUBLICATIONS

Marblehead, MA

Copyright ©1997
by Circuit Publications
PO Box 1201
Marblehead, Mass. 01945
All rights reserved.

02 01 00   TS 6 5 4 3 2

The text of this publication, or any part thereof, may be reproduced for use in classes for which *Teaching the Language of Time* is the text. It may not be reproduced in any manner whatsoever for any other purpose without prior written permission from the publisher.

ISBN: 0-923573-25-9

TABLE OF CONTENTS

Introduction v

Sequenced Facts

Before, matching 1
Present time, regular occurrence,
    personal experience 2
Before, personal experience 4
After, personal experience 6
Sequence, simple events 8
Sequence, complex events 16
Before, during, after, support page 34
Prefix *pre-*, suffix *post-* support page 35

Time Factors that Influence Events

When meaning under certain conditions 36
When/conditions worksheets 40
Concurrent events, concept, discussion 42
Concurrent events, support pages 46

"Pieces of Time;" Talking About Time Measurement

"Pieces of Time," introduction 49
Parts of a clock 50
Clock, vocabulary review 51
Morning, afternoon 52
Evening 53
What time is it? (the hour) 54
What time is it? (past the hour) 55
What time is it? (the half hour) 56
What time is it? (before the hour) 57
What time is it? support page 58
Days in a week 59
Days, weeks in a month 60
Months in a year 62
Years and events in centuries 64
Events that occur periodically 67
Pieces of time, review; visual representation 68

Cycles, Schedules, Comparing Past/Present, Rates of Speed

Events that occur in cycles, introduction 69
Seasons as parts of a cycle 70
Events in nature which occur in cycles 71
Scheduled events, introduction 75
Personal schedule 76
Team sport schedule 77
Bus schedule, driver's point of view 78
Bus schedule, passenger's point of view 79
Schedule, support pages 82
Comparing past/present, introduction 84
Comparing past/present events, support pages ... 86
Rate of speed, introduction 92
Rate of speed, support page 93

Personal Time; Age, Timeline of One's Life

Ages of people, introduction 94
Ages of people, support pages 96
Personal timeline 102
Time vocabulary review-crossword puzzle 104
Answers to word searches, crossword puzzle, and
    some support page questions 105

Introduction

The language of time is an important part of a child's language development program. We are constantly experiencing the influence of time concepts in our daily lives. Order of events, quantities of time, simultaneous events and time-based contingencies are pervasive aspects of our lives. We arrange our personal lives in response to schedules; we are influenced by events occurring in cycles; we remember past and plan future events; always operating within various time frames: we are influenced by time concepts.

Learning--success in school--depends on grasping time concepts. Understanding history and seeing how history influences our lives today depends on understanding past events in chronological order. Understanding how events occurring in sequence impact each other is important in studies of history as well as science. Time factors are most important in studying the Earth and its life forms. Understanding concepts such as animals becoming extinct, live plants and animals becoming fossils or substances changing form under time-related conditions require a firm grasp of temporal operations. Success in dealing with math concepts involving time/distance/rate relationships is based on understanding how time concepts overlay spatial concepts and concepts of motion. Most classroom presentations and discussions in some way involve the language of time.

Time concepts and relationships develop as we grow in maturity and experience. For most of us, the language of time attaches itself to these emerging concepts; time concepts broaden as our experience grows and we continually acquire new language. For example the word *early* starts out as a very concrete event in the mind of a young child--perhaps a parent coming home from work *early* or being *early* for a pediatrician's appointment, thus having time to play with the toys in the office. *Early* becomes associated with particular quantities of time--being ten minutes *early* is not a big a quantity as being an hour *early*. We discuss *early* settlers of a country, *early* innings of a baseball game, *early*-blooming flowers, *early* returns of an election or "*early*-bird specials" at a department store. This one word finds its way into our lives and our learning by many different paths, leaving its impression on concepts and ideas that we grow up with.

The ability to operate with in-depth knowledge of terms denoting time concepts enables us to make correct associations as we observe events surrounding us. The development of this language challenges our language-impaired students. The language of time, because it is associated with abstract relational concepts, might also elude students who are learning English as a second language. Of course our students experience time-related events, but they might lack the language needed to fully understand and express time concepts and relationships. Helping our students acquire the language of time is helping them to participate in learning new information and in seeing relationships among facts and ideas. Devoting language lessons to particular time concepts and related language is a very worthwhile investment in a student's overall learning experience.

We must be prepared to answer questions as to our students' understanding of time concepts and language. We must constantly check our students' knowledge of time concepts and language as we present information which we assume that they understand.

Those of us who intervene in students' grammar or syntax development work to teach progressively more complex sentences. We work to teach relative clauses and many embedded messages using carefully constructed phrases. As we move along the syntax development trail, we must determine that our students have the cognitive basis for each grammatic form that we teach. For example, as we teach phrases or clauses such as *while we were driving* (something happened) or *when it rains* (something happens), do we know that our student understands the concept of simultaneous events?

Do young children understand basic concepts and language of sequential events before they learn about dinosaurs and other prehistoric animals? Do elementary students know the impact and own the related language of time-related occurrences effecting the ecology of our environment? Do we know that students challenged by complex math problems understand the concepts and language of simultaneous events occurring in dynamic relationships to each other?

As language specialists, we have opportunities to explain and demonstrate the significance of language as it impacts students' overall learning. More and more speech/language pathologists find themselves in collaborative and inclusion-type settings in schools. We have many chances to explain and demonstrate how "talking through" events and relationships helps students learn complex concepts. Because of our deep understanding of language and its impact on our thinking, we know how to break down experiences and express each step in manageable language. We should be doing this and demonstrating this for other educators. If our young students approach learning by "talking through" relational concepts such as those of temporal and ordinal relationships, they will become much better thinkers. Their young minds will be far more receptive to understanding and expressing the more complex ideas of reason and logic awaiting them in later grades. I hope that this book gives you some ideas and helps you present the language of time to your students and your colleagues.

The book...

... presents a number of time-related concepts and corresponding language. It is intended to be used to teach the language of time to students of many ages. The first part of the book presents simple time-related ideas from a child's own personal experience. This is followed by simple, then complex sequential events. Here you will find activities for young children including pictures and support pages.

Following are sections presenting a variety of time concepts and language. Immediately following the sections dealing with sequenced events is a section that focuses on the idea of events occurring when particular circumstances prevail. This is followed by a section presenting ideas about concurrent events.

The next section deals with "pieces" of time--from seconds and minutes all the way to centuries. Here concepts of identifying and measuring time as it passes are presented. The pages in this section offer many activities for students to talk about the quantities of time that are represented on clocks and calendars.

Following this is a section presenting schedules. This section offers many ideas that your students probably experience in their own lives. Next is a section devoted to the idea of events that occur in cycles. Comparing past and present events is presented next, followed by a section on the concept of rate of speed. In these sections, you might develop ideas about showing time relationships in history as well as science.

Finally, personal time is addressed once again. A section dealing with various aspects of ages of people is presented. These pages suggest a way for students to develop time-lines of their own lives.

Susan and I hope that this book helps you bring the language of time to the forefront of your students' language development programs--and that you enjoy doing so!

Marilyn

Sometimes it's important to do something before you do something else. Match the questions on the left with the answers on the right.

1. What must you do before you walk on a clean floor?

2. What must you do before you go out in the cold?

3. What must you do before you cross the street?

4. What must you do before you ride your bike?

5. What must you do before you eat dinner?

6. What must you do before you cut your birthday cake?

7. What must you do before you go to bed?

8. What must you do before you go to school in the morning?

a. Take a bath.

b. Put on your warm coat.

c. Blow out the candles.

d. Look both ways.

e. Wash your hands.

f. Wipe your shoes.

g. Put on your helmet.

h. Eat a good breakfast.

What happens when you're at school?

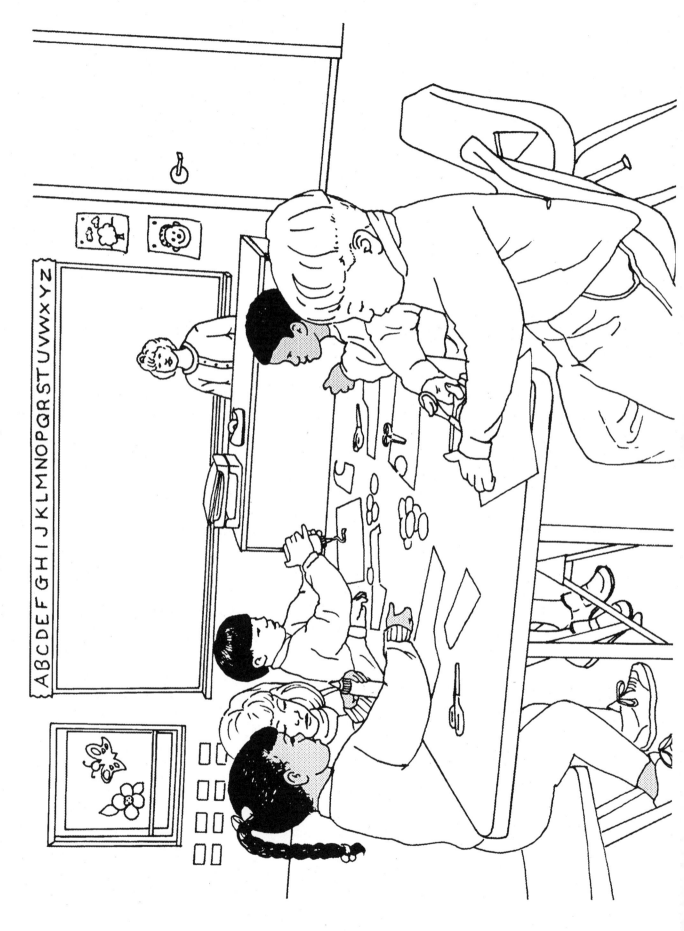

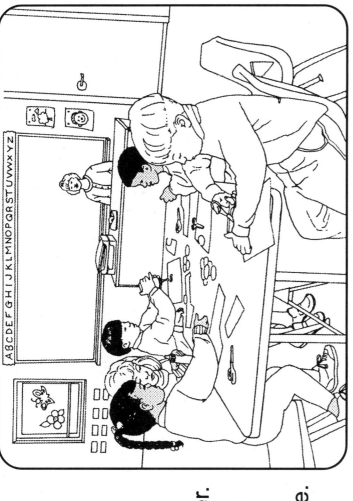

Talk about the people who are doing things at school. Point to each person or people as you tell what they are doing.

1. This boy is cutting.
2. This girl is holding a bottle of glue.
3. This boy is talking to another boy.
4. These girls are sharing the glue.
5. This boy is pouring glue on his paper.
6. The teacher is watching the children work.
7. These children are sitting at the table.
8. This teacher is sitting at the desk.

Talk about what you are doing now.

1. Are you sitting down now?
2. What kind of room are you in now?
3. Talk about some things you can see around you.
4. What can you hear if you listen now?
5. Who else is in this room now?

Words to help tell what is happening: now, today, is, am, are, doing, has

©Circuit Publications *Teaching the Language of Time*

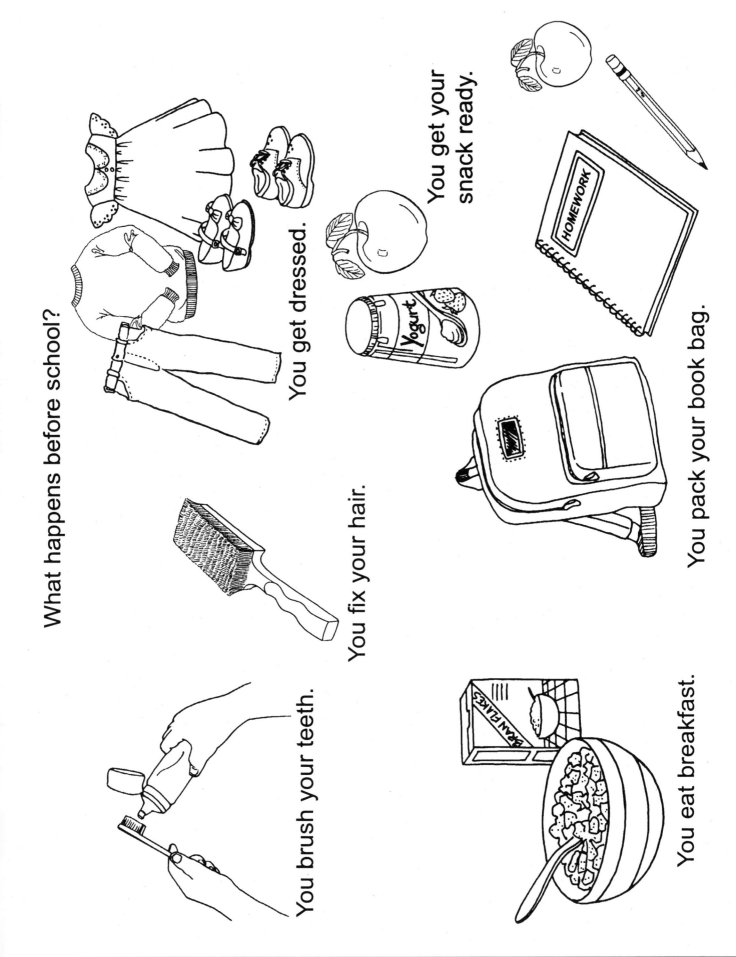

Talk about what you do before school.

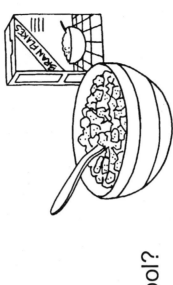
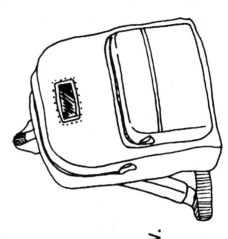

1. Do you get dressed before school?
2. Do you brush your teeth before school?
3. Do you brush your hair before school?
4. Do you eat breakfast before school?
5. Do you get your books ready before school?
6. Do you get your lunch or snack ready before school?
7. Do you think about what you will do at school?
8. Do you think about the friends you will see at school?
9. Talk about some things you will do before school tomorrow.

Words to help tell what will happen: before, tomorrow, will do, will have, plan, prepare

What happens after school?

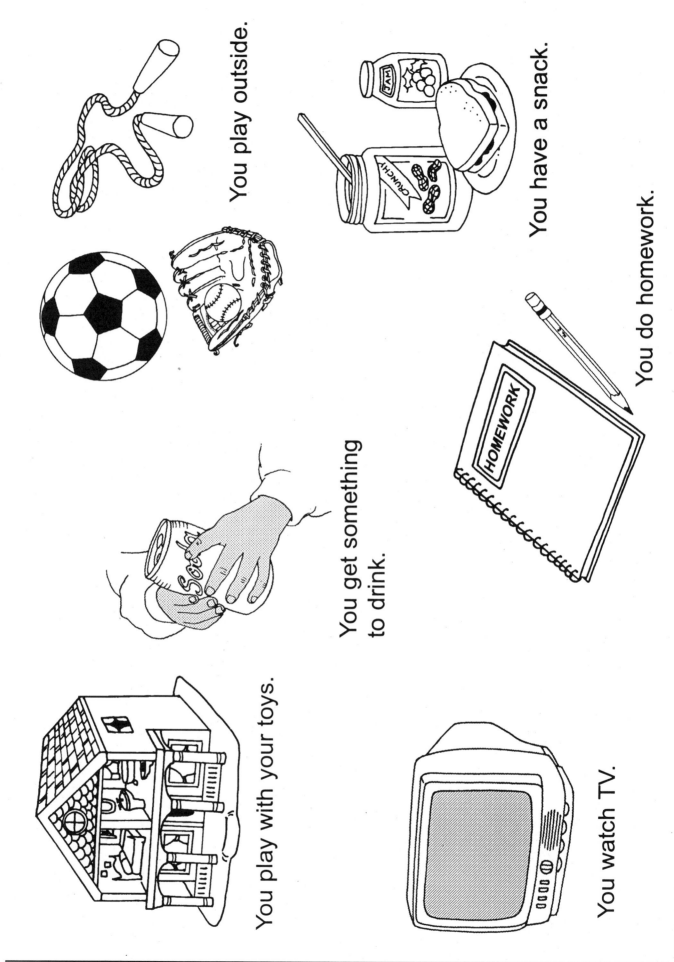

You play outside.

You have a snack.

You do homework.

You get something to drink.

You play with your toys.

You watch TV.

Talk about what you do after school.

1. Do you do your homework after school?

2. Do you have a snack after school?

3. Do you play with your toys after school?

4. Do you play outside after school?

5. Do you watch TV after school?

6. Do you show Mom and Dad something you made at school?

7. Do you see your friends after school?

8. Do you have dinner after school?

Words to help tell what happened: did, after, had, was, were, remember

First

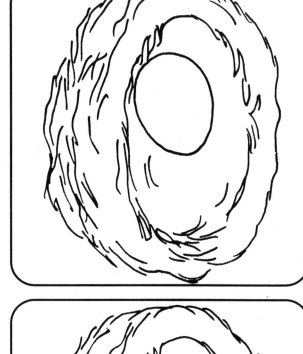

Next

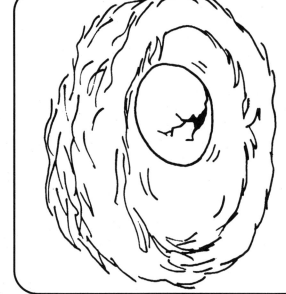

Last

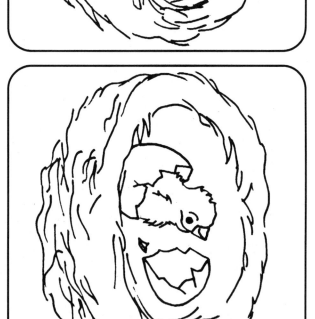

1. What happened first?

2. What happened next?

3. What happened last?

4. What happened while the egg was in the nest?

5. What happened before the egg cracked?

6. What happened after the egg cracked?

7. What will happen after the baby bird grows bigger and stronger?

Teaching the Language of Time

First   Next   Last

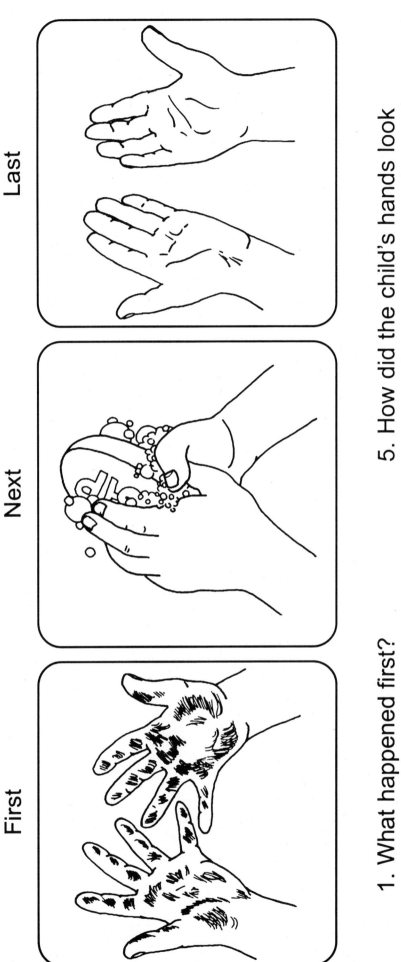

1. What happened first?

2. What happened next?

3. What happened last?

4. How did the child's hands look before they were washed?

5. How did the child's hands look after they were washed?

6. What was happening to the dirt while the child was washing her hands?

©Circuit Publications   *Teaching the Language of Time*

First

Next

Last

1. What happened first?

2. What happened next?

3. What happened last?

4. How did the snowman look before it started to melt?

5. How did the snowman look after it had melted?

6. Why was the snowman melting?

First   Next   Last

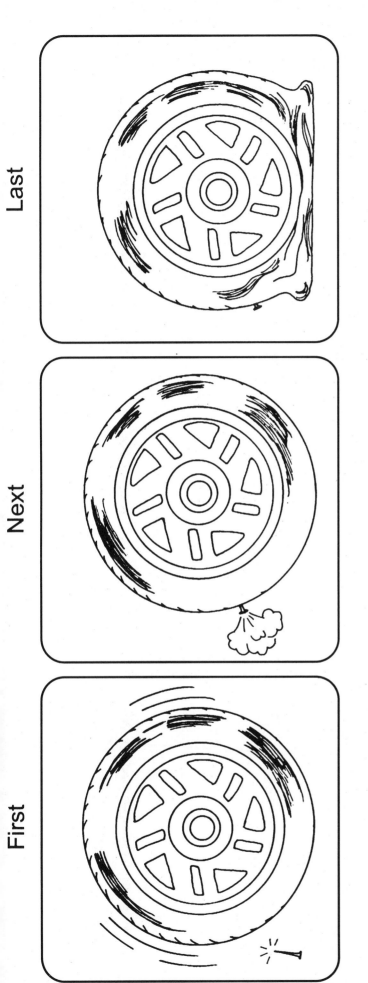

1. What happened first?

2. What happened next?

3. What happened last?

4. Tell how the tire looked before the nail made a hole in it.

5. What is happening in the middle picture?

6. Tell how the tire looks in the last picture. Why does it look like this?

©Circuit Publications   *Teaching the Language of Time*

First

Next

Last

1. What happened first?

2. What happened next?

3. What happened last?

4. Tell how the pitcher looks in the first picture.

5. What is happening in the second picture?

6. Tell why the pitcher looks different in the first and last pictures.

7. When is the pitcher the emptiest? When is it the fullest?

Teaching the Language of Time ©Circuit Publications

First **Next** **Last**

1. What happened first?

2. What happened next?

3. What happened last?

4. Tell how the man's face looked before he shaved.

5. What is happening in the middle picture?

6. Tell how the man's face looks in the last picture. Why does he look different here than he looked in the first picture?

©Circuit Publications *Teaching the Language of Time*

Look at these pictures. Each one shows something happening, but the pictures are out of order. Write numbers 1, 2 or 3 below each picture to show the correct order.

 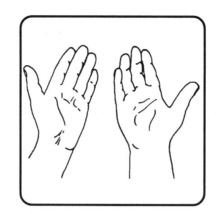 

_____   _____   __1__

_____   _____   _____

What happens first, next and last when you go to school?

_____ ride the bus to school

__1__ get on the bus

_____ get off the bus

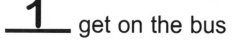

What happens first, next and last when you brush your teeth?

_____ put your toothbrush away

_____ brush your teeth

__1__ put toothpaste on your toothbrush

Look at these pictures. Each one shows something happening, but the pictures are out of order. Write numbers 1, 2 or 3 below each picture to show the correct order.

_____   _____   **1**

  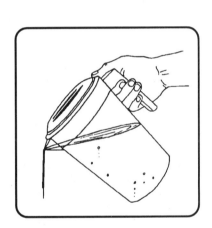

_____   _____   _____

What happens first, next and last when you make a sandwich?

_____ put 2 pieces of bread together

_____ cut the sandwich in half

1 spread the peanut butter and jelly on the bread

What happens first, next and last when you put your shoes on?

_____ put your shoes on

1 put your socks on

_____ tie your shoes

The following pages are presented for you to help children thoroughly focus on a complex event such as a birthday party and the time relationships of simpler events within.

Complex events, a birthday party, a family dinner, a camping trip and building a new house are presented, each with the following components:

a narrative presentation of the event

a full-page picture of the central point of the event

1 or more support pages intended as a paper/pencil task

9 smaller pictures, 3 showing what happens before, 3 during and 3 after

Here are some suggestions for using these pages:

Children should first be shown the full-page picture and discuss the event. For example, have them describe the birthday party as they see it. They should be encouraged to share information from their own experiences and ideas.

The small picture cards can then be used in many ways. Children should think about and discuss some things that happen *before*, *at* or *during*, and *after* a party.

Children can sort the cards according to time, learning to classify events in this way. Or they can use them to discuss the order of events which strengthens their understanding and use of the words *before* and *after*.

These activities might also be used to help children talk about planning their own special events, such as class projects or parties. They should learn to identify preparation and follow-up activities with something that they will do. For students who need help organizing their own activities, presenting concepts of *before*, *during* and *after* in this simple way can be helpful.

Finally, the written support page or pages provide students with something to take home and share with parents.

Pam's birthday party

Pam's birthday was last week. She wanted to have a small party at home to celebrate her birthday.

Before the party, she called her best friends, Carol, Lee and Michael and invited them. She went shopping with her dad and bought special hats, cups and other party things. Then she and her mom decorated the house for the party.

At the party, Pam and her friends had a great time. Pam blew out the candles on her cake. Everyone played with their party toys. Pam opened her presents.

After the party, Pam said good-bye  to her friends. She helped her mom clear the table and put the cake away.

Pam's Birthday Party

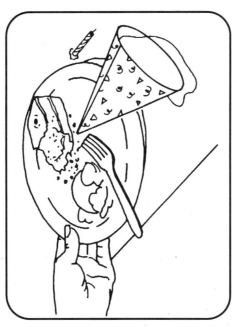
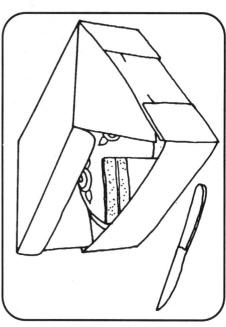
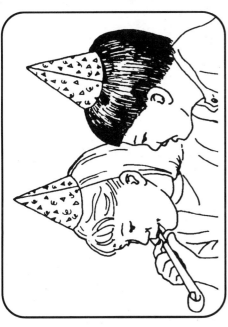

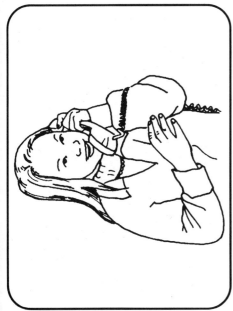
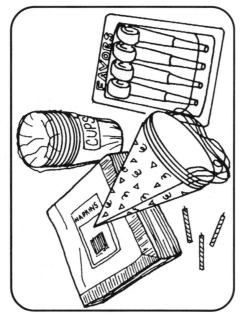
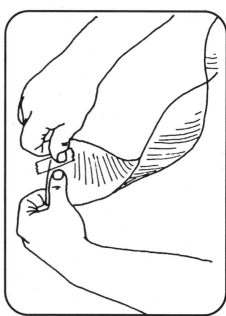

Teaching the Language of Time

Read each question. Think about when you would do these things. Use the words **before** and **after** to help you answer the questions.

1. When do you buy party things?

I buy things _____ the party.

2. When do you say good-bye?

I say good-bye _____ the party.

3. When do you decorate your house?

I decorate _____ the party.

4. When do you invite your friends?

I invite them _____

Think about what happened before and after Pam's birthday party. Circle the words **before** and **after** in these sentences.

Pam called her friends before the party.

Before the party, Pam bought special hats.

Pam's friends went home after the party.

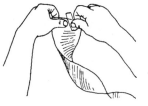

Pam made decorations before the party.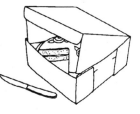

After the party, Pam put the cake away.

Pam helped Mom clear the table after the party.

The Johnsons' Dinner

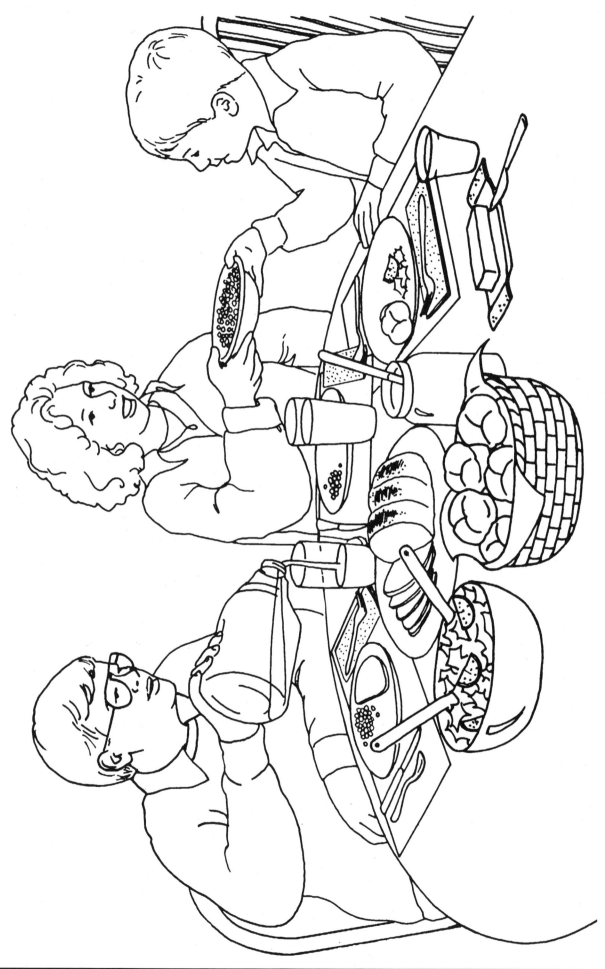

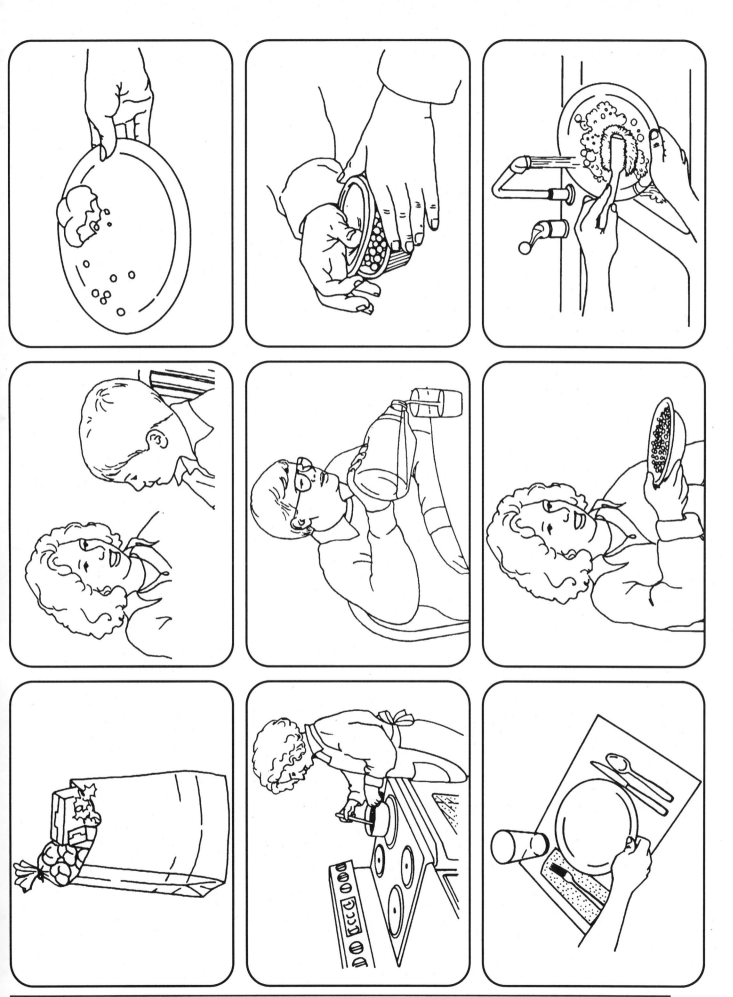

Teaching the Language of Time 23

The Johnsons' Dinner

Every Sunday the Johnsons have a special dinner.

Before dinner, Mr. Johnson and his son Calvin go to the store and buy the food. Mrs. Johnson cooks the dinner. Calvin sets the table.

While they eat their dinner, they talk about things that are important to them. They pass the food to each other and pour their juice. The Johnsons always enjoy their good food. They also enjoy talking to each other and sharing their ideas.

After dinner, they clear the plates from the table. Mom puts the leftover food away. Dad and Calvin wash the dishes.

Think about what happened before and after the Johnsons' dinner. Circle the words **before** and **after** in these sentences.

1. Mr. Johnson and Calvin went shopping before dinner.

2. Mom cooked the food before dinner.

3. After dinner, everyone cleared the table.

4. Mom put away the left-overs after dinner.

5. Before dinner, Calvin set the table.

6. Dad and Calvin washed the dishes after dinner.

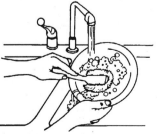

The Camping Trip

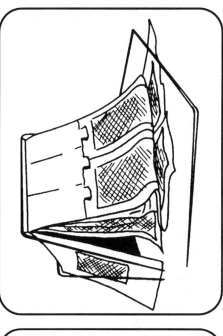
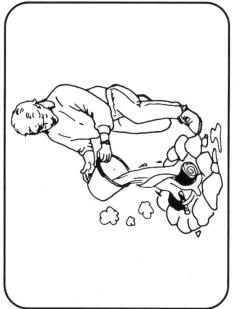
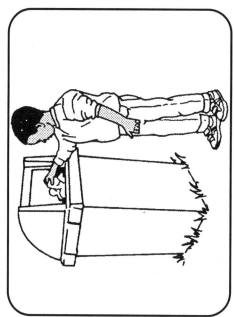

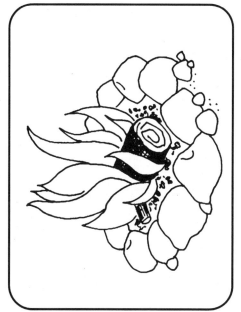

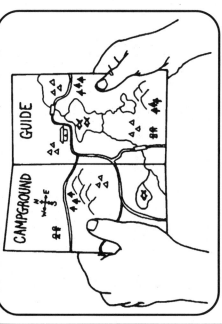

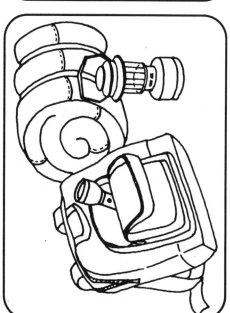

The Neighbors' Camping Trip

Last summer, some friends from Gail and Correys' neighborhood went on a camping trip.

Before the trip, the grown-ups looked at a map and chose a nice campground. The children helped gather their camping gear. Each family packed their food in a large cooler.

While they were camping, they enjoyed being outdoors. They put up tents.  They hiked in the woods each day. They made fires to cook and to help them keep warm each evening. They cooked their food on the fire.

At the end of the camping trip, everyone got ready to go back home. They took their tents down. They carefully put out their  campfires. They threw their trash away.

Think about what happens before and after the camping trip. Circle the words **before** and **after** in these sentences.

1. The grown-ups planned the trip and looked at a map before they went camping.

2. They got their camping gear ready before the trip.

3. After camping, they threw away their trash.

4. Just before the trip, everyone packed their food in a cooler.

5. They took their tents down after they had finished camping.

6. They put the campfire out after they camped.

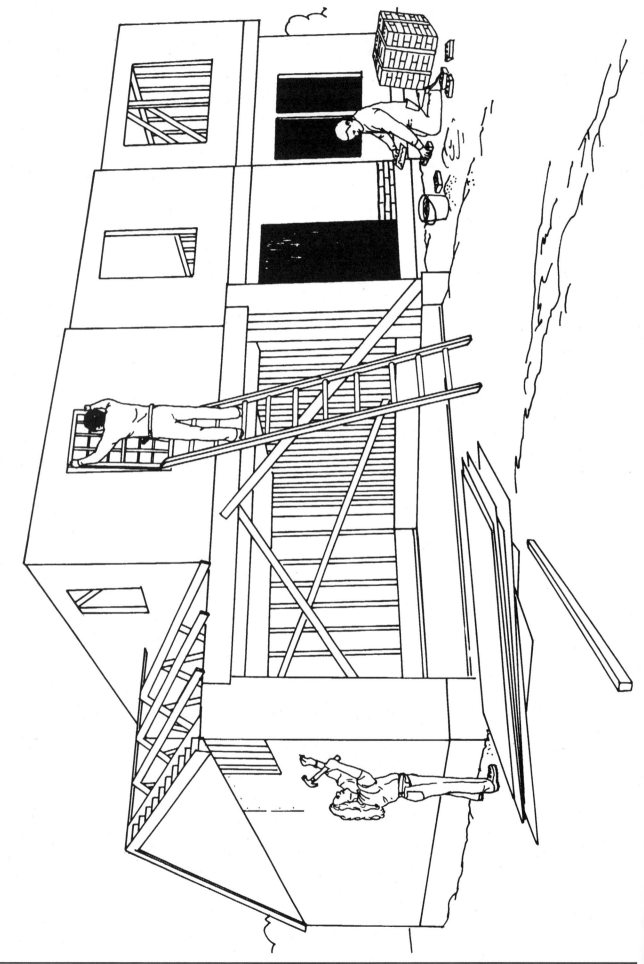

Building a New House

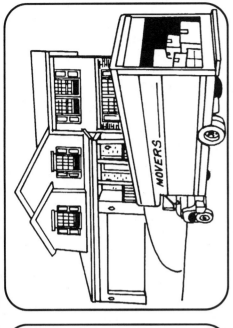 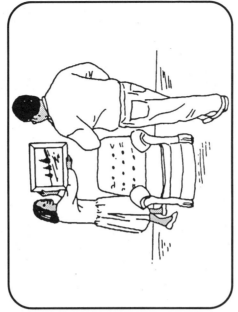 
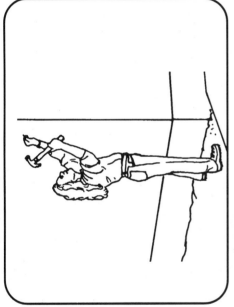 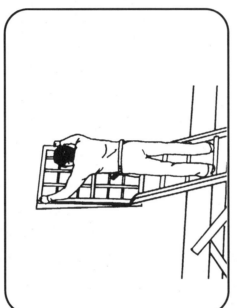 
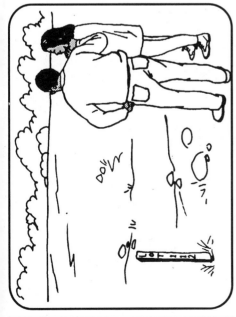 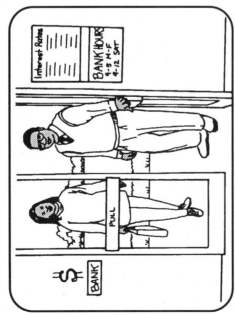 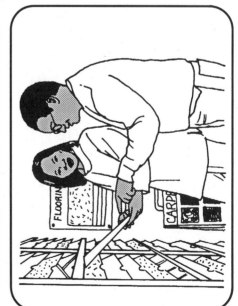

Teaching the Language of Time

Building a New House

Deanna and James decided to build a new house.

There were many things to do before their house was built. Deanne and James found a beautiful lot where the house would be built. They went to the bank to borrow the money they would need. They picked out paint, wallpaper and tile for their new house.

Soon the builders were busy building the house. They poured concrete, nailed boards together and laid bricks. They put in windows and doors. They put on the roof and painted the house.

After the house was built, James and Deanna moved in. They put their things just where they wanted them in their new house. They planted grass and flowers outside.

Read the questions about Deanna and James' new house. Use the words **before** and **after** to help you answer each question.

1. When did James and Deanna find a place to build the house?
   They found a place _____ the house was built.

2. When did they plant grass and flowers?
   They planted things _____ the house was built.

3. When did they borrow money to build the house?
   They borrowed money _____ the house was built.

4. When did they choose paint and wallpaper?
   They chose these things _____ the house was built.

5. When did they move in?
   They moved in _____ the house was built.

What would someone do **before**, **during** and **after** each of these events?
Use your imagination!

1. What would someone do before he planted flowers?
   What would he do while he was planting the flowers?
   What would he do after he had planted the flowers?

2. What would you do before a big snow storm?
   What would you do during the storm?
   What would you do after the storm was over?

3. What would your family do before they had a yard sale?
   What would they do during the yard sale?
   What would they do after the yard sale was over?

4. If you were a soccer player, what would you do before a soccer game?
   What are some things you might do during the game?
   What would you probably do after the game?

5. What would you do before you went on your dream vacation?
   What would you do while you were on this vacation?
   What would you do after the vacation was over?

6. If you were a race car driver, what you do before a big race?
   What are some things you would do while you were driving in the race?
   What would you do after the race was over?

7. What would your family do before you moved into a new house or apartment?
   What would you do while you were moving?
   What would you do after you were all moved in?

8. If you were an actor and had a big part in a play, what would you do before the play?
   What would you do while you were acting in the play?
   What would you do when the play was over?

9. What would you do if you were going to get a new puppy?
   What would do when you went to get your puppy?
   What would you do after you brought your new puppy home?

10. If you were an artist, what you do before you painted a picture?
    What do you think you would do while you were painting this picture?
    What would you probably do after you had finished the painting?

The prefix **pre-** tells us that a word refers to something that happened before an event. The prefix **post-** says this word refers to something that happened after an event. Think about the meaning of each of these words. Use some of these words to fill in the blanks in the sentences below.

prearrange	preoperation
prebake	preholiday
preseason	prestamp
precut	pretrial
preelection	pretax
prefrozen	pretest

postwar	postgame
posttest	postelection
posttax	postnatal
postdelivery	postoperative
postarrest	postgraduate

1. The announcer said, "Be sure to stay tuned for the _____ show which will be broadcast immediately after this football game."

2. Our teacher gave us a _____ before we studied this chapter so she could find out how much we knew already.

3. My brother's _____ pay is much better than his _____ pay. That's because a lot of money is taken out of his pay for taxes.

4. My uncle had his shopping done way ahead of time and saved a lot of money because he bought all his holiday gifts at the _____ sale at the shopping mall.

5. Grandpa had to go to the hospital for a _____ examination the day before his surgery.

6. We didn't have to cut these decorations out before we put them up because they were _____ when we bought them.

7. My sister graduated from college last year but she went back to school to get a _____ degree.

8. My mom has to leave the meeting early because she has some _____ work to do do before her client's trial begins tomorrow.

9. I don't believe everything this candidate says. I think he is just making _____ promises so that people will vote for him.

10. Our hometown basketball team will play two _____ games the week before the season actually begins.

11. Officer McCracken had to finish some _____ procedures after he questioned and arrested the suspect.

12. The cake has been _____ so all we have to do is cut it and eat it!

©Circuit Publications *Teaching the Language of Time* 35

When it snows, it's a special time! Think about the things you do when it snows. Finish each sentence using your own ideas.

1. When it snows, I can _____.

2. When it snows, I like to _____.

3. When it snows, I feel _____.

4. When it snows, I wear _____.

5. When it snows, I call _____.

6. When it snows, I want _____.

7. When it snows, I have _____.

8. When it snows, I play with _____.

9. When it snows, I see _____.

10. When it snows, I listen to _____.

11. When it snows, I pretend _____.

12. When it snows, I don't _____.

13. When it snows, I can't _____.

14. When it snows, I wish _____.

When it's sunny, and hot it's time for fun outside. Finish each sentence using your own ideas.

1. When it's hot and sunny, I go _____.

2. When it's hot and sunny, I feel _____.

3. When it's hot and sunny, I wear _____.

4. When it's hot and sunny, I like to eat _____.

5. When it's hot and sunny, I like to drink _____.

6. When it's hot and sunny, I call _____.

7. When it's hot and sunny, I play with _____.

8. When it's hot and sunny, I should _____.

9. When it's hot and sunny, I pretend _____.

10. When it's hot and sunny, I can't _____.

11. When it's hot and sunny, I have _____.

12. When it's hot and sunny, I don't like _____.

13. When it's hot and sunny, I wish _____.

When it rains, it's not a good time to go outside. Finish each sentence using your own ideas.

1. When it rains, I feel _____.

2. When it rains, I stay _____.

3. When it rains, I wear _____.

4. When it rains, I call _____.

5. When it rains, I play with _____.

6. When it rains, I see _____.

7. When it rains, I hear _____.

8. When it rains, I like to _____.

9. When it rains, I don't like _____.

10. When it rains, I pretend _____.

11. When it rains, I have _____.

12. When it rains, I want _____.

13. When it rains, I can't _____.

14. When it rains, I wish _____.

When I'm sick, it's not a happy time. Finish each sentence using your own ideas.

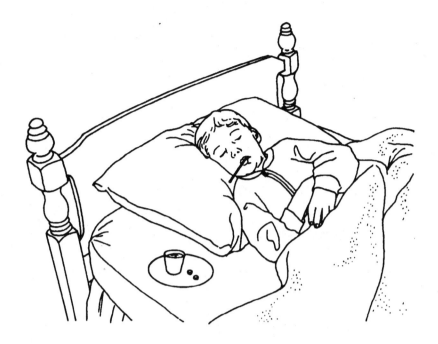

1. When I'm sick, I feel _____.

2. When I'm sick, I can't _____.

3. When I'm sick, I have to _____.

4. When I'm sick, I like _____.

5. When I'm sick, I don't _____.

6. When I'm sick, I eat _____.

7. When I'm sick, I drink _____.

8. When I'm sick, I have _____.

9. When I'm sick, I wear _____.

10. When I'm sick, I should _____.

11. When I'm sick, I don't want _____.

12. When I'm sick, I wish _____.

Answer each question telling when and under what conditions or circumstances these things might happen.

1. When would you hear a siren?
2. When does someone mow her lawn?
3. When does a dog bark?
4. When would you need sunglasses?
5. When would someone need to wear a tuxedo?
6. When does someone win a gold medal?
7. When do you need to buy a present?
8. When do you go to the dentist?
9. When can you open your windows?
10. When should the windows be closed?
11. When are schools closed during the winter?
12. When do you ask a question?
13. When do we have a new president?
14. When do birds fly south?
15. When does a cat purr?
16. When do blossoms grow on trees?
17. When do you begin to prepare for your favorite holiday?
18. When does a war end?

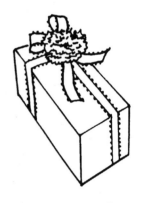

Think about things that happen or that Kevin does (on the left side of the page). Then, think about what happens when these things occur (on the right side of the page). Draw a line connecting the related events.

1. When Kevin didn't eat breakfast,
2. When Kevin's uncle drove too fast,
3. When Kevin was late for school,
4. When Kevin didn't water his garden,
5. When Kevin made the basketball team,
6. When Kevin didn't study,
7. When Kevin was sick,
8. When it rains,
9. When Kevin's birthday comes on a Saturday,
10. When Kevin loses his lunch pass,
11. When Kevin dials 911,
12. When Kevin's dog gets a rabies shot,
13. When Kevin opens the windows,
14. When Kevin's dad drove over a nail,
15. When Kevin's team won the game,
16. When Kevin's washing machine breaks down,
17. When Kevin misbehaves in school,
18. When Kevin's ball hit the window,
19. When Kevin sets his clock for 7 o'clock,

a. it broke.
b. he got a flat tire.
c. he didn't get a good grade on his test
d. he can't eat lunch at school.
e. he felt hungry in the morning.
f. the coach took the players out to celebrate.
g. Kevin needs an umbrella.
h. it rings at 7 o'clock.
i. he had to go to the office and get a tardy slip.
j. he got a detention.
k. he had to practice twice a week and be at all the games.
l. a police officer comes right over.
m. he got a speeding ticket.
n. Kevin isn't afraid that she'll get rabies.
o. the plants dried up and died.
p. he went to the doctor.
q. Kevin's family has to go to the laundromat.
r. he can't bring treats to school on his birthday.
s. there is a nice breeze.

©Circuit Publications — Teaching the Language of Time

Different events are happening at the same time.

While these people are traveling in an airplane...

...these children are standing next to a building in their town looking up in the sky at the airplane!

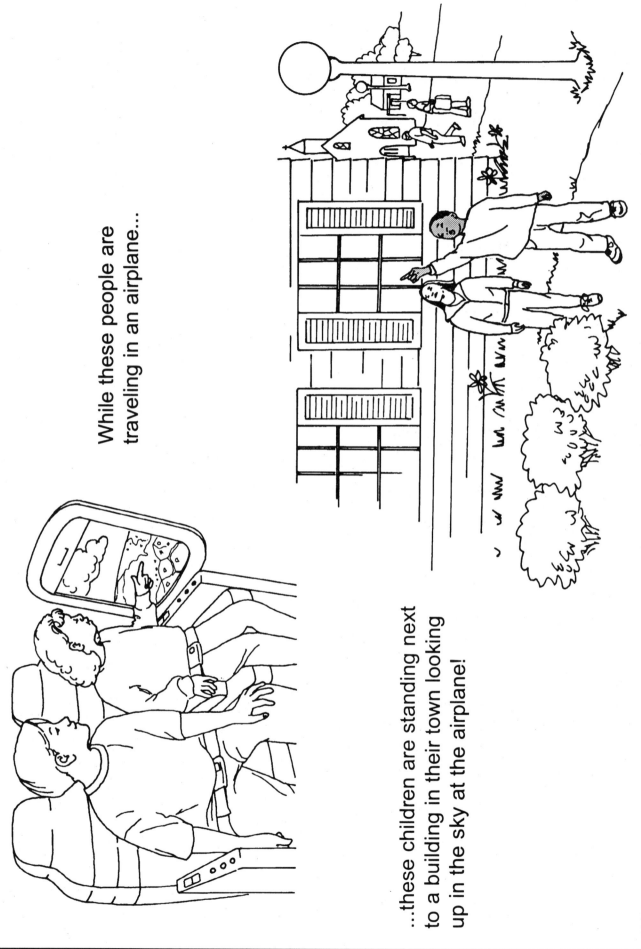

Think about what is happening in the airplane and what is happening in the town at the same time.

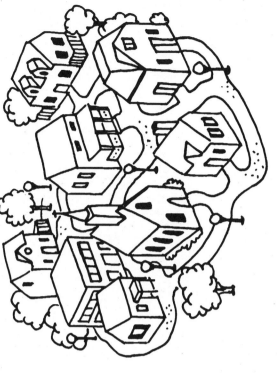

In the airplane:

1. What is the pilot doing? Who can the pilot talk to? What must the pilot watch? What would the pilot do if it becomes windy and the ride becomes bumpy?

2. What are the passengers doing? What are they doing for their safety? What happens when it's dinner time and the passengers get hungry? What are some things the passengers can see out of their windows?

In the town:

1. What are the children doing?

2. What do you think the grown-ups are doing at home?

3. What is happening in some of the stores?

4. What might be happening at the church?

5. What special events might be happening in the town today?

6. What would the people in the town see if they looked up in the sky?

©Circuit Publications   *Teaching the Language of Time*

Different events are happening at the same time.

While these people are cheering for their town's baseball team...

...the batter is getting ready to swing at the ball and hit a home run.

Think about what is happening with the baseball fans and what is happening with the baseball players at the same time.

1. This young man is a great baseball fan. He comes to the games as often as he can. Sometimes he watches the games on TV. He always reads about his team in the sport section of the newspaper. What is he hoping this team will do?

2. The fans really want their team to win this game. Why is this important?

3. What else will happen if the batter hits the ball over the fence for a home run?

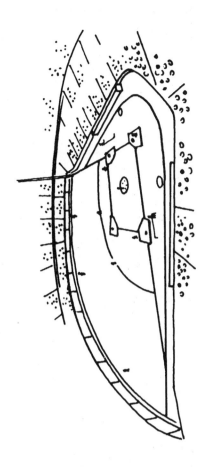

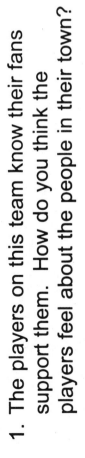

A home run here would be great - we'd win for sure! If our Sox beat these Yankees we'll get into the playoffs!

1. The players on this team know their fans support them. How do you think the players feel about the people in their town?

2. What will they hear if this batter hits a home run?

3. What will they see if they look up at their fans as a home run ball goes over the fence?

Talk about things that happen at the same time that something else is happening. Begin each sentence with the underlined phrase and complete the sentence using your own ideas.

Think about what is happening while you're working at school.

<u>While I'm working at school</u>:

- my mom is...
- my dad is...
- my friends are...
- my teacher is...
- the principal is...
- the cafeteria workers are...
- people are driving their cars down the street in front of my school. Maybe they are...

Think about what is happening while you're asleep at night. Some people work at night doing important jobs for their businesses, towns or cities. Some animals sleep all day and are awake at night. Places look different at night than they do during the day. Finish these sentences saying what you think is happening while you are sleeping at night.

<u>While I'm sleeping</u>:

- owls are...
- the night watchman at the bank is...
- workers at the morning newspaper are...
- the sun...
- very early in the morning, the baker...

What are some things you, your family or friends do while riding in a car, on a train, on an airplane or--use your imagination--in a rocket ship?

<u>While I'm riding</u>:

- in a car, I...
- on a train, I...
- on an airplane, I...
- in a rocket ship, I...

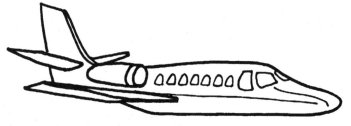

Teaching the Language of Time

Sometimes two or more things are happening at the same time. Think about all the things that are going on just as each of these special events is about to take place. Answer these questions.

1. A new show is about to open at your town's community theater. The first performance is tomorrow night.
    - What are the actors doing?
    - What are the workers doing to get the theater ready?
    - What is happening at the ticket box office?
    - What are the people in town who will go to the show thinking about and doing?

2. The Red Sox are going to play in the first game of the World Series this afternoon, in just two hours.
    - What are the ball players doing?
    - What are the workers doing to get the stadium ready?
    - What are the radio and TV broadcasters doing?
    - What are the fans who will go to the game doing?

3. The senior class at the high school will graduate this Sunday. Imagine that today is the Friday before graduation.
    - What are the graduates doing?
    - What are the teachers and school staff doing to get everything ready? (the school auditorium, programs, diplomas, flowers, caps and gowns, speeches, many other things)
    - What are the graduates' families doing to get ready for their celebrations?

4. Jonathan and Paula are getting married this afternoon at six o'clock. Imagine that it's now four o'clock.
    - What do you think Paula and her bridesmaids are doing?
    - What are Jonathan and his groomsmen doing?
    - What are all the people who are needed for the wedding ceremony and celebration doing? (parents, minister or rabbi, caterer, florist, photographer, band, drivers, many more!
    - What are the guests doing?

©Circuit Publications   *Teaching the Language of Time*

In each of these places, different things were going on at the same time. Read each group of sentences. Tell which one does not belong because it tells of something that could not have been going on at the same time as the others.

1. At the zoo:
    - The workers were feeding the lions and tigers their mid-day meal.
    - Children and grown-ups were walking around looking at the animals.
    - The moon and stars shone brightly.

2. At the beach:
    - The lifeguard sitting high up on his seat slowly glanced from one side to the other making sure all swimmers were safe.
    - Dark clouds moved across the sky as lightning flashed and thunder roared.
    - Sara turned her back to the sun as she stretched out on her towel watching her little cousins build their sand castle.

3. At the restaurant:
    - The painters were moving the tables and chairs out of the dining room so they could begin their work.
    - The workers hustled about in the kitchen preparing fresh salads and sauces for the evening meal.
    - The manager was posting the dinner specials near the entrance.

4. At school:
    - The custodian was checking the furnace for the last time before he went home for the night.
    - The fingerpaintings that the kindergarten children had done that afternoon lay drying on the tables in the dark, empty classroom.
    - The principal was announcing that there would be indoor recess because it was starting to rain.

5. In the ship:
    - The captain was steering slightly to the north in order to avoid the storm that was coming toward them.
    - The school children stood in line waiting to tour the ship.
    - The sailors who had been out on deck began to come down into the ship because the sea was getting rough.

6. At the house:
    - Ms. Kennedy put the mashed potatoes into a nice bowl and the vegetables into silver serving dishes.
    - Ms. Kennedy carefully arranged the centerpiece on the table and placed a linen napkin at each of the eight places.
    - The firefighters removed their hoses and fire extinguishers from the house feeling satisfied that the fire was out and no one had been injured.

8. At the sports arena:
    - The coach talked to the players in the locker room before they entered the arena for the championship basketball game.
    - The workers drove the Zamboni machine around the ring to make the ice smooth for the hockey game.
    - The excited basketball fans anxiously waited for the teams to come onto the court and play the championship game.

How do we talk about pieces of time?

We count seconds, minutes and hours so we know how much time has gone by each day. We count days, weeks and months so we know how much time has gone by each year.

We use a clock to count seconds, minutes and hours.

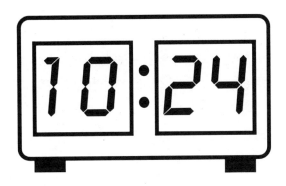

We use a calendar to count days, weeks and months.

MARCH						
SUN	MON	TUE	WED	THU	FRI	SAT
1	2	3	4	5	6	7
8	9	10	11	12	13	14
15	16	17	18	19	20	21
22	23	24	25	26	27	28
29	30	31				

This clock shows the numbers 1 - 12, the second hand, the minute hand and the hour hand. Also, see the dots around the inside edge of the clock. The numbers mark the hours, the dots mark the seconds and the minutes.

Each day has 24 hours. The first part of the day is called morning. Morning begins at 12:00 midnight and ends at 12:00 noon. The second part of the day is called afternoon and evening or night. This part begins at 12:00 noon and ends at 12:00 midnight. There are 12 hours in the morning and 12 hours in the afternoon and evening or night. A day ends and a new day begins at 12:00 midnight.

The second hand goes all the way around the clock each minute. The minute hand goes all the way around the clock each hour. The hour hand goes all the way around the clock the first part of the day, 12 hours, and the second part of the day, 12 hours. There are 24 hours in one day.

This is a clock too. It's called a **digital clock**. The number on the left of the : shows hours. The number on the right of the : shows minutes. A digital clock usually does not show seconds.

Think about the words that help us talk about how much time has passed each day. Think about the words and ideas that help us talk about clocks. These words will help you answer the questions below.

minute
hour
second
morning
afternoon
12 o'clock
midnight
12 o'clock noon

second hand
minute hand
hour hand
numbers
afternoon or evening
morning
digital clock

1. How many hours are in a full day?

2. What is the first part of the day called?

3. When does afternoon begin?

4. When I look at a clock, what tells me how many hours have gone by?

5. How do I know how many minutes have gone by?

6. What part of a clock goes all the way around each minute?

7. When does a day end?

8. When does a day begin?

9. What is the second part of the day called?

10. Do you remember how many seconds are in a minute? How many minutes are there in an hour? If you counted all the dots around the outer edge of the clock, how many dots would there be? Why?

11. What kind of clock is this?

12. Does a clock tell you whether the time that it shows is morning or evening? Why?

The new day begins at 12 o'clock, midnight. The hours between 12 o'clock midnight and 12 o'clock noon are the morning hours. The afternoon begins at 12 o'clock. Afternoon becomes evening and evening becomes night. The day is over at 12 o'clock midnight. What do you do at different times of the day?

In the morning...
- What do you do when you first wake up?
- What are some things you do in the morning before you go to school?
- What time does your class have lunch and recess?
- What are some special things you do in the mornings on weekends, Saturday or Sunday mornings?

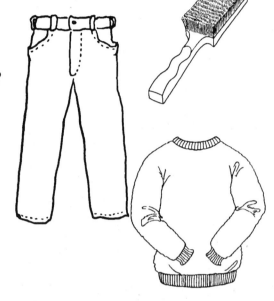

In the afternoon...
- How do you know when to say, "good morning" or "good afternoon?"
- What time does your class come back from lunch or recess?
- What are some things you usually do in the afternoon at school?
- What special things do you do in school on some afternoons?
- What time does school end?
- What are some things you do in the afternoon after school?
- What special things might you do in the afternoon on Saturdays or Sundays?

Teaching the Language of Time

There is no particular time when afternoon ends and evening begins. It might be different for different people or in different parts of the world.

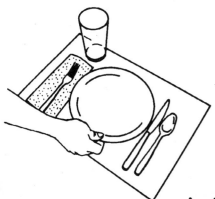
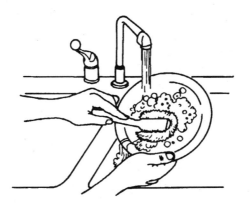

In the evening...
- When do you and your family eat dinner?
- When do your mom or dad get home from work?
- What are some things that you and your family do in the evening or at night?
- What are some special things you might do in the evening when there's no school the next day?
- What time do you usually go to bed?
- What do you do just before you go to bed?
- Do you get to stay up late when there's no school the next day?

When do *you* think evening begins?

The hands on the clock tell us how many hours and minutes have gone by since the morning or the afternoon began. The hour hand (smaller hand) points to the number of hours that have passed. At the end of any hour and the beginning of the next hour the minute hand is pointing to twelve.

Example: What time is it?

It is nine o'clock.

Here are some clocks that show how many hours have passed since 12 o'clock midnight or 12 o'clock noon. When we tell what time it is we say the number of the hour that ended and "o'clock."
Point to each clock and answer the question, "What time is it?"

As an hour passes, the minute hand moves forward from 12 all the way around the clock and back to 12. Then the next hour begins. The hour hand tells us how many hours have passed since 12:00 midnight or 12:00 noon. The minute hand tells us how many minutes have passed during an hour that is passing. The digital clock shows the same time as the other clock. When you tell what time it is you tell how many hours have passed since midnight or noon, and how many minutes have passed since the hour began.

Example:
    What time is it?
        It's 5 minutes after 9.
or... It's 5 minutes past 9.
or... It's 9:05.

These clocks show that 5 minutes have passed since 9 o'clock.

What time is it?
    It's _____
or... It's _____
or... It's _____

This clock shows that 10 minutes have passed since 3 o'clock.

What time is it?
    It's _____
or... It's _____
or... It's _____

This clock shows that 20 minutes have passed since 7 o'clock.

What time is it?
    It's _____
or... It's _____
or... It's _____

This clock shows that 25 minutes have passed since 10 o'clock.

These two clocks show that 30 minutes have gone by since 9 o'clock. Thirty minutes is half as many minutes as sixty, the number of minutes in an hour. If we tell someone that thirty minutes have passed we say:

"It's nine-thirty."
or... "It's half (an hour) past nine."
or... "It's 9:30."

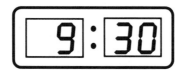

Point to each clock and answer the question, "What time is it?"

Teaching the Language of Time

This clock shows that more than thirty minutes have passed since 9 o'clock. When more than thirty minutes or half an hour has gone by, we often say how many minutes must go by before the next hour.

Example:
   What time is it?
   It's 20 minutes until 10.
or... It's 20 minutes before 10.
or... It's 40 minutes after 9.
or... It's 9:40.

These clocks show that 40 minutes have passed since 9 o'clock. It will be 10 o'clock in 20 minutes.

What time is it?
   It's _____
or... It's _____
or... It's _____
or... It's _____

This clock shows that 50 minutes have passed since 2 o'clock.

What time is it?
   It's _____
or... It's _____
or... It's _____
or... It's _____

This clock shows that 35 minutes have passed since 1 o'clock.

What time is it?
   It's _____
or... It's _____
or... It's _____
or... It's _____

This clock shows that 55 minutes have passed since 4 o'clock.

Think about words and sentences that say what time it is. The sentences on the left side of the page tell what time is shown on the clocks on the right. Draw a line from each clock to the sentence telling what time it shows.

1. This clock shows that ten minutes have passed since seven o'clock.

2. This clock shows half passed two.

3. This clock shows twenty-five minutes until six o'clock.

4. This clock shows that forty minutes have passed since three o'clock.

5. This clock shows fifteen minutes before five o'clock.

6. This clock shows ten ten.

7. This clock shows one fifteen.

8. This clock shows the end of a day and the beginning of a new day.

58   *Teaching the Language of Time*   ©Circuit Publications

There are seven days in one **week**. The days always come in the same order.

Sunday	first
Monday	second
Tuesday	third
Wednesday	fourth
Thursday	fifth
Friday	sixth
Saturday	seventh

first → JANUARY ← seventh

Sun	Mon	Tue	Wed	Thur	Fri	Sat
					1	2
3	4	5	6	7	8	9
10	11	12	13	14	15	16
17	18	19	20	21	22	23
24	25	26	27	28	29	30
31						

The day happening now is today. The day before today is called yesterday. The day after today, the next today, will be tomorrow. Use the words **yesterday**, **today** and **tomorrow** to finish these sentences or answer the questions.

1. Today is Monday. What will tomorrow be?

2. Yesterday was Monday. What will tomorrow be?

3. Tomorrow is Friday. What day was yesterday?

4. Yesterday was Thursday. What was the day before yesterday?

5. Today is Sunday. What will the day after tomorrow be?

6. Yesterday was Monday. What will the day after tomorrow be?

7. Tomorrow is Tuesday. What will the day after tomorrow be?

8. Today is Saturday. What day will it be in two days?

9. Yesterday was Wednesday. What day will come two days after tomorrow?

10. What was the day before yesterday if the day after tomorrow is Friday?

11. It was Tuesday two days ago. What day was yesterday?

12. The day after tomorrow is Sunday. What day will tomorrow be?

13. It was Monday two days ago. What day will tomorrow be?

©Circuit Publications — Teaching the Language of Time

May

Sunday	Monday	Tuesday	Wednesday	Thursday	Friday	Saturday
				1 book report due	2	3 baseball game
4	5 school pictures	6 baseball practice	7 trumpet lesson	8 dentist 4:00 math test	9	10
11 Mother's Day	12 firefighter's visit	13 baseball practice	14 trumpet lesson	15	16 Puffy - vet 4:00	17 baseball game
18 Ted's birthday party	19	20 baseball practice	21 trumpet lesson	22 get Grandma and Grandpa	23 pick up iron	24 family picnic
25	26 Memorial Day	27 baseball practice	28 trumpet lesson	29	30	31 ZOO

Here is a page from Randy's calendar showing the month of May. Notice the days Sunday through Saturday lined up along the top. This first day of this month is a Thursday. The last day of the month is a Saturday. There are four weeks and three days in May. Each day of May is marked with a number. The first day of May is Thursday, May 1. The last day is May 31.

> When we tell or write the date, the day which something happened, we use the name of the month and the number of the day.

Randy uses his calendar to remind him of special things that will happen. What are the dates that each of these things happen this month?

1. On what day will school pictures be taken?

2. When is Mother's Day?

3. When is Randy's book report due?

4. What is the date of Memorial Day?

5. What day each week does Randy have baseball practice?

6. How many trumpet lessons does Randy have in May? What are the dates of his trumpet lessons?

7. Randy's baseball team plays their first two games in May. When do they play their first game? What is the date of their second game?

8. Randy will be going to his cousin Ted's birthday party in May. When is this party?

9. When will a firefighter come to school and talk to Randy's class?

10. One day, Randy's mom took their iron to the repair shop to be fixed. She was told that the iron would be ready in 10 days. When should Mom pick up the iron? When did she take it to the repair shop?

11. When will Randy take his cat to the vet?

12. Randy and his friends will go to the zoo on the last day of the month of May. What date is this?

13. Randy and his mom will pick his grandparents up at the airport on May 22. There will be a big family picnic two days later. What is the date of the family picnic?

14. Randy's dad plans to build some shelves in Randy's room during his vacation, the third week in May. He said that everything must be out of Randy's room three days before he starts to build the shelves. When must Randy take everything out of his room?

©CIRCUIT Publications   *Teaching the Language of Time*   61

A **year** has 12 months. January is the first month, December is the twelfth or last month. There might be 28, 30 or 31 days in one month. Here are the months, as they will occur in the year 1999.

		JANUARY				
S	M	T	W	T	F	S
					1	2
3	4	5	6	7	8	9
10	11	12	13	14	15	16
17	18	19	20	21	22	23
24	25	26	27	28	29	30
31						

		FEBRUARY				
S	M	T	W	T	F	S
	1	2	3	4	5	6
7	8	9	10	11	12	13
14	15	16	17	18	19	20
21	22	23	24	25	26	27
28						

		MARCH				
S	M	T	W	T	F	S
	1	2	3	4	5	6
7	8	9	10	11	12	13
14	15	16	17	18	19	20
21	22	23	24	25	26	27
28	29	30	31			

		APRIL				
S	M	T	W	T	F	S
				1	2	3
4	5	6	7	8	9	10
11	12	13	14	15	16	17
18	19	20	21	22	23	24
25	26	27	28	29	30	

		MAY				
S	M	T	W	T	F	S
						1
2	3	4	5	6	7	8
9	10	11	12	13	14	15
16	17	18	19	20	21	22
23	24	25	26	27	28	29
30	31					

		JUNE				
S	M	T	W	T	F	S
		1	2	3	4	5
6	7	8	9	10	11	12
13	14	15	16	17	18	19
20	21	22	23	24	25	26
27	28	29	30			

		JULY				
S	M	T	W	T	F	S
				1	2	3
4	5	6	7	8	9	10
11	12	13	14	15	16	17
18	19	20	21	22	23	24
25	26	27	28	29	30	31

		AUGUST				
S	M	T	W	T	F	S
1	2	3	4	5	6	7
8	9	10	11	12	13	14
15	16	17	18	19	20	21
22	23	24	25	26	27	28
29	30	31				

		SEPTEMBER				
S	M	T	W	T	F	S
			1	2	3	4
5	6	7	8	9	10	11
12	13	14	15	16	17	18
19	20	21	22	23	24	25
26	27	28	29	30		

		OCTOBER				
S	M	T	W	T	F	S
					1	2
3	4	5	6	7	8	9
10	11	12	13	14	15	16
17	18	19	20	21	22	23
24	25	26	27	28	29	30
31						

		NOVEMBER				
S	M	T	W	T	F	S
	1	2	3	4	5	6
7	8	9	10	11	12	13
14	15	16	17	18	19	20
21	22	23	24	25	26	27
28	29	30				

		DECEMBER				
S	M	T	W	T	F	S
			1	2	3	4
5	6	7	8	9	10	11
12	13	14	15	16	17	18
19	20	21	22	23	24	25
26	27	28	29	30	31	

Answer these questions about the months in a year. Use the calendar of the year 1999 on page 62.

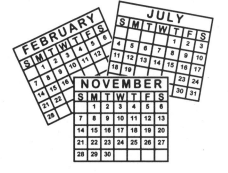

1. How many months have 30 days?

2. How many months have 31 days?

3. Which month has only 28 days?

4. What is the third month of the year?

5. What is the third last month of the year?

6. Which month comes between June and August?

7. If someone's birthday came in February and he had to wait four months before he got his birthday gift, when would he get his gift? How do you know?

8. Shelly's birthday is in October. She is sad because her best friend moved away six months before her birthday so Shelly isn't able to celebrate her birthday with her best friend. When did Shelly's friend move away? What did you do to answer this question?

9. Mitch's uncle from Montana came to visit in February. He said he'd be back in three months. When can Mitch expect his uncle to come back? How do you know this?

10. Mr. Sawyer must have his project finished by the end of the year. If he had five months left in which to finish the project what month would it be now? How did you figure this out?

11. Gwen must travel from Boston to Los Angeles every other month starting in June until the end of the year. How many trips will she make? How do you know?

©Circuit Publications   *Teaching the Language of Time*   63

A **century** is 100 years. Here are lists of important things that happened in each century beginning with the year 1000. Events that happened in the years from 1 to 1000 are in the first two lists. Note that many things happened throughout the world before the year 1.

Before 5th Century
- Cities in many parts of the world formed
- Near and Far East, North, South America, Asia, Africa, Europe
- People traveled on horses, in ox-driven carts or carried by servants
- Great Wall of China built
- Outdoor theaters established in Greece
- Paddle-wheel boats used
- Paper discovered
- Shirt- and coat-like garments worn
- Music (hymns) sung in churches, trumpets played in Greece, early string instruments in India, oboe in Rome

5th to 10th Centuries
- Cities continued to develop around the world
- American Indians built early towns. Some grew corn and squash and developed ways of irrigating their crops
- Iceland discovered
- Numerals as we use them today first used
- Citizens voted to choose their leaders in Greece
- Silk and cotton fabrics used
- Glass windows appeared
- Gold jewelry worn
- Coins used as money
- Egyptian mummies buried
- Large orchestras played in China

1000's
- More cities developed
- First clock used
- First Christmas carol sung in German

1100's
- Large churches built in Europe
- Windmills used
- American Indians build pueblo homes
- Engagement rings first used
- Tower of Pisa built
- Love songs performed by French troubadours

1200's
- Large colleges founded in Europe
- Spectacles (eye glasses) invented
- Great Mali Empire founded in Africa

1300's
- Ming Dynasty begins in China
- Bubonic plague spreads in India
- Bastille built in France
- Spinning wheel invented
- Sawmill invented
- Playing cards used
- Distance measurement established by an English king
- Trade fairs took place in Europe
- Weaving began
- Tennis first played in England
- Lute a popular musical instrument
- Religious leaders forbid certain kinds of music

1400's
- European cities grew larger
- First lottery played
- Math symbols (+ and - first used)
- First black lead pencil used
- Parachute invented
- Some sports forbidden by English king (football, golf, bowling)
- Printing press used
- Music written for ballet
- Columbus sailed to the Americas

1500's
- Horse-drawn carriages first used
- European explorers explored the Americas
- Slaves brought to the Americas
- Pocahontas was born
- da Vinci painted the Mona Lisa
- First dictionary published
- Shakespeare's plays first performed
- Chocolate first enjoyed in Spain
- Sugar crops first planted
- Rubber discovered
- Fork first used
- First violins made

1600's
- Many African kingdoms existed; people farmed, did metal and cloth work, enjoyed art and music
- Santa Fe settled; the first settlement in America
- Isaac Newton explained gravity
- Europeans came to settle in the Americas
- Destruction of Indians began in the Americas
- Coffee became a popular drink in Europe
- Ice cream became popular dessert in Europe
- Peter the Great became Russia Czar
- Harvard College founded in America
- Harp, French horn, recorder, flute used in concerts
- Opera houses built in Europe
- Stagecoach first used

1700's
- French Revolution fought
- American Revolution fought
- American colonies declared independence
- First steam engine built
- Newspapers started in America
- Thermometer invented
- First encyclopedia printed
- Famous symphonies composed (Handel, Bach, Mozart, Beethoven)
- First piano made

1800's
- Napoleon's armies invaded Europe
- Slavery ended in America
- Steam engine used in trains and ships
- Electricity discovered
- Telephone invented
- Radio invented
- First car built
- Louis Pasteur discovered that germs cause disease
- Morse code, telegraph invented
- First professional sports team (Cincinnati Red Stockings) established
- Beautiful music written by Tchaikovsky--Nutcracker Suite

1900's
- Many electric conveniences appeared in everyday life
- World Wars I and II fought
- Many European nations' borders changed following wars
- Madame Curie recognized for discoveries in atomic science
- Psychoanalysis developed by Sigmund Freud
- Airplane invented
- Atomic bomb dropped by USA in Japan
- United States grew to 50 states
- First movies shown
- Television invented
- Ballpoint pen invented
- Computers invented
- Outer space explored
- Many special people in our lives born!

During a century, 100 years, many things happen. We identify a century by referring to the number that will be reached on the last day in the last year of that century.

As the last day of the last year of the current century ends 2,000 years (20 centuries or 20 x 100 years) a new day, a new year and a new century begins. During the 1900's, the world is in the twentieth century according to our calendar. During the 2000's, the world is in the twenty-first century.

In what century was each of the following years?

1950	1248	1898	1066	126
1521	746	1329	1492	987
1101	1004	1177	1975	621
1876	39	579	1	479

Refer to the lists of events in centuries on pages 64 and 65. Answer these questions.

1. In what century did Christopher Columbus sail to the New World?

2. When was an engagement ring first used?

3. When did the Greeks elect their leaders?

4. In what century did the Ming Dynasty in China begin?

5. When were spectacles (eye glasses) invented?

6. In what century was the Mona Lisa painted?

7. Windmills were first used in the same century that the Tower of Pisa was built. What century was this?

8. Which instrument was used first, the piano or the trumpet? In which century were these instruments first used?

9. In which century did the French and the American revolutions take place?

10. Was the radio invented in the same century as television?

11. How many centuries went by between the time when the stagecoach was first used and when the car was invented?

12. In what century were you born?

Teaching the Language of Time ©Circuit Publications

Some things occur regularly-every day, (daily), every week (weekly), etc. Some things occur twice or three times in a period. The prefix *semi-* tells us that something occurs twice in a period. The prefix *bi-* means two and says that something happens every other period.

Here are some words that tell us how often something occurs. Use these words to fill in the blanks in these sentences.

```
daily ------------------- -every day
weekly --------------- -every week
monthly -------------- -every month
yearly ---------------- -every year
annually ------------- -every year
bimonthly ----- -once every two months
semiannually   - - - -two times each year
biennial ------ -once every two years
centennial ------ -once every century
```

1. Grandpa's golf magazine comes each month. It is a _____ magazine.

2. Toni is supposed to prepare _____ reports for her supervisor. She prepared these reports in March and May. When is the next report due?

3. Alice and her cousin deliver their town's _____ paper in their neighborhood every Thursday.

4. James' doctor told his mother that James must take one pill _____ and that he should come back to see him when the medicine is gone. James' mother bought a bottle containing 14 tablets for James at the pharmacy. She made an appointment for him to return to the doctor in two weeks.

5. My mom's _____ business convention will take place in about three months, around the middle of February.

6. Zach gets a _____ bonus check, once in the spring and once in the autumn.

7. We will have a grand _____ celebration in our town in 2007 to celebrate its 100th birthday.

8. Ted and his little sister go to the doctor each summer for their _____ physical exam.

9. My favorite _____ TV show comes on at eight o'clock on Thursdays.

10. Dad got _____ paychecks on February 28 and March 31. He has to budget the money carefully so it will last until April 30.

These are words used to talk about exact "pieces" or divisions of time. Large pieces of time can be broken down into smaller ones. A second is the smallest amount of time that we usually talk about.

A year has 12 months

A month has 4 weeks

A week has 7 days

A day has 24 hours

An hour has 60 minutes

A minute has 60 seconds

If this block represents a time of one year...

...a decade would have 10 years or blocks,

...and a century would have 100 years or blocks,

... and a millennium would have 1000 years or blocks.

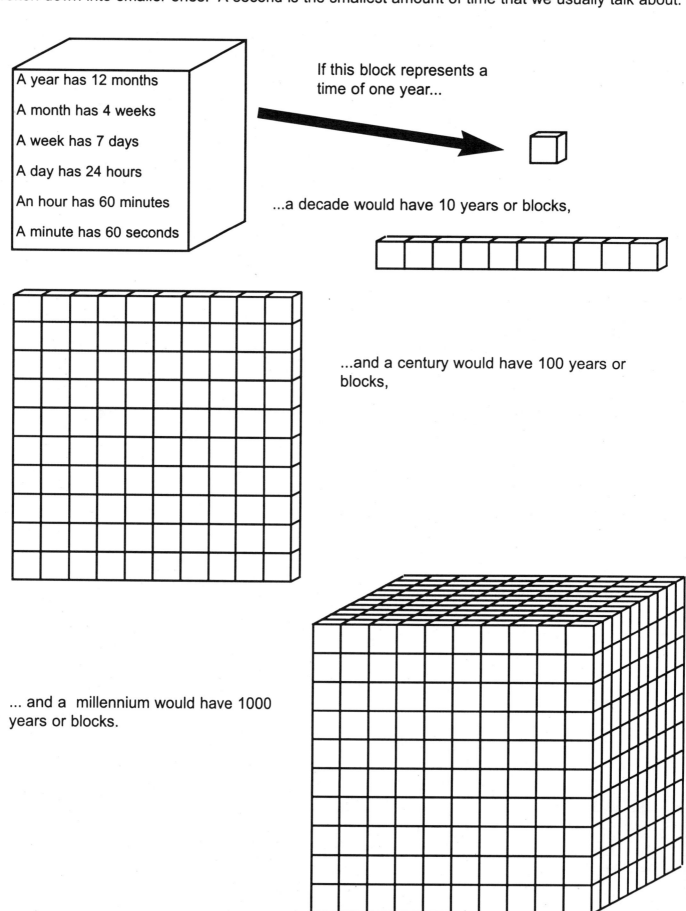

68   *Teaching the Language of Time*   ©Circuit Publications

When things happen over and over again in the same order and return to the starting point, we call this a cycle. When a **cycle** occurs, there is a beginning point of the cycle, (movement from the beginning toward the end of the cycle) and the point when the cycle ends and the new cycle begins.

1. The **cycle** begins
2. The **cycle** moves forward
3. The **cycle** ends and a new cycle begins

A day is a cycle.

A new day begins at 12 o'clock midnight.

The morning hours pass.

The morning ends and the afternoon and evening begin at 12 o'clock noon.

The afternoon and evening hours pass.

The day ends and a new day begins at 12 o'clock midnight.

A year is a cycle. Tell why.

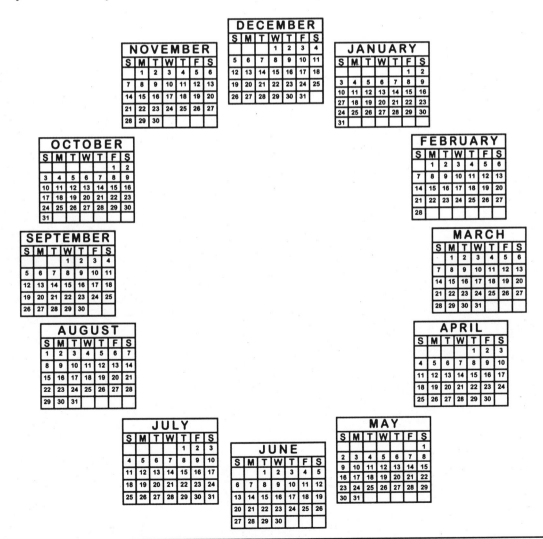

The **seasons**, spring, summer, autumn and winter occur in a **cycle**.

Spring is the season when many new things begin to grow.

In the **summer** many plants bloom and produce fruit during warm sunny days.

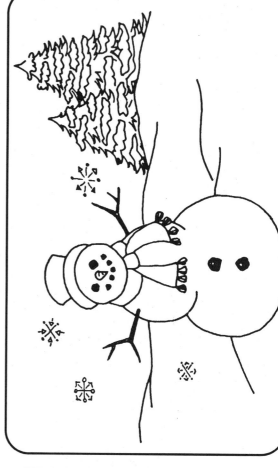

Autumn is the season when most plants are fully mature. They are beginning to end their growing season and rest.

Winter is the season when most plants are not growing. They are resting, getting ready for the new beginnings of spring.

Answer these questions about the seasons.

In the spring:

1. What kind of weather do you experience?
2. What kind of clothes do you wear?
3. What are some things you like to do?
4. What do you notice about trees and plants around you?
5. What do you know about animals in the spring?
6. When does spring begin? When does it end?

In the summer:

1. What kind of weather do you experience?
2. What kind of clothes do you wear?
3. What are some things you like to do?
4. What do you notice about trees and plants around you?
5. What do you know about animals in the summer?
6. When does summer begin? When does it end?

In the autumn:

1. What kind of weather do you experience?
2. What kind of clothes do you wear?
3. What are some things you like to do?
4. What do you notice about trees and plants around you?
5. What do you know about animals in the autumn?
6. When does autumn begin? When does it end?

In the winter:

1. What kind of weather do you experience?
2. What kind of clothes do you wear?
3. What are some things you like to do?
4. What do you notice about trees and plants around you?
5. What do you know about animals in the winter?
6. When does winter begin? When does it end?

Why do we say that the seasons occur in a cycle?

Think about the **cycles** that the lives of these animals, robins and salmon follow.

Robins let us know that winter is ending and spring is beginning every year! This is when they return from the warmer climate in the southern parts of North America where they have spent the winter.

Soon after they arrive they build nests for the mother birds to lay their eggs. The eggs are laid and hatched. Mother and father birds gather insects and berries to eat and to feed their babies. When the baby birds grow big and strong enough, they can fly away.

Robins stay in their northern homes during the spring and summer. When the summer turns to autumn and the days get cold, robins will fly far away, back to places in the southern part of North America where it is warm. They stay in these nice warm places all winter, then return to the north in the spring.

Salmon are fish which live in the seas in the northern hemisphere. When salmon become adults they are ready to lay eggs (ready to spawn). They swim from the sea to rivers and keep swimming up-river until they reach the same streams where they were spawned and hatched.

Sometimes their journey is hundreds of miles long. They might swim through waterfalls and rapids, some very difficult conditions, in order to return to their birthplace.

When they return to the streams where they were hatched, their eggs are spawned, fertilized and hatched. The young salmon will then stay in these freshwater streams for several months, up to a year. When they are strong enough to swim back down to the sea, they grow up there and become adults.

Think about the **cycles** that the lives of these plants, apple trees and tomato plants follow.

There are many different kinds of apples, but they all grow on trees. The apple tree's branches are bare during the winter. The tree is resting, waiting for the new growing season to begin in the spring.

As winter turns to spring, tiny new leaves begin to grow on the branches. When the leaves are growing but still tiny, about 1/2 inch long, apple buds grow inside the leaves.

The leaves grow bigger and bigger. The buds grow into beautiful blossoms. Hundreds or even thousands of blossoms cover the tree in the spring. The blossoms stay for a while, then fall to the ground leaving only the center of the blossom. This tiny bud slowly grows into a tiny green apple.

As spring turns to summer and summer passes, these tiny green apples grow bigger and begin to turn red. As summer turns into early autumn, the apples become ripe and ready to pick and eat. As autumn passes, the leaves on the apple tree turn from green to autumn colors.

Then they fall from the tree. All winter the branches are once again bare. Now the tree rests and waits for the new growing season to begin.

Tasty, juicy tomatoes are wonderful parts of salads or sandwiches. The plants on which they grow come from their own seeds!

In the spring, tomato seeds are planted. As spring passes, days and nights become warmer and tiny tomato plants come up through the ground. These plants grow bigger as blossoms sprout. These blossoms fall off, leaving tiny green tomatoes on the branches.

As the warm, sunny summer days pass, the tomatoes grow bigger and begin to turn red. When the tomatoes are red and ripe, they are ready to pick and eat. If you save some of the seeds from your tomato, you can plant them next spring and grow your own tomato plants!

Talk about the **cycles** that the lives of animals and plants follow. Answer these questions about robins, salmon, apple trees and tomatoes.

What do robins do in the early spring, the beginning of their year's cycle?
What do robins do during the different seasons of a year?
When does a new cycle in the robin's life begin?

When does a salmon's life cycle begin?
What do salmon do from the time they are hatched to the time that they are adults?
What do adult salmon do as they get ready to spawn giving life to new baby salmon?

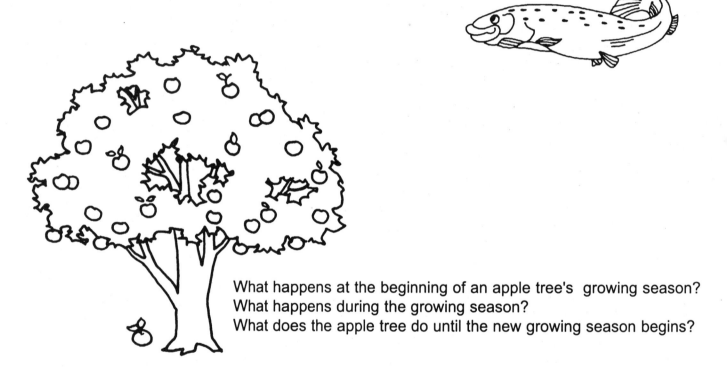

What happens at the beginning of an apple tree's growing season?
What happens during the growing season?
What does the apple tree do until the new growing season begins?

What happens at the beginning of the life cycle of a tomato plant?
What happens between the time the seeds are planted and the tomatoes are picked and eaten?
What is the end of the tomato plant's cycle?

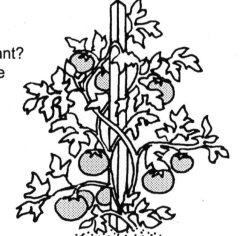

Teaching the Language of Time

A schedule is a plan that lists the time and order that a group of events take place.

Here is Matt's daily schedule. Matt follows this schedule each day that he goes to school. On week-ends and during school vacations, his daily schedule is different.

TIME	ACTIVITY
7:00	Matt wakes up and gets ready for school
7:45	He gets on the school bus
8:15	He arrives at school and gets ready for morning classes
8:45	Matt's first class, math begins
9:45	Math class ends, language arts class begins
10:45	Matt's class has a morning recess break
11:00	Social studies class begins
12:00	The students go to the cafeteria for lunch
12:25	Lunch recess begins, students go to the playground
12:50	Recess ends, students return to their classroom
1:00	Science class begins
2:00	Students have a study period
2:30	School ends; Mark gets on the school bus
3:00	Matt returns home
4:00	Matt goes to an activity or team sport practice
5:00	Matt returns home and begins his homework
6:00	The family has dinner
6:30	Matt finishes his homework
8:30	Matt gets ready for bed

Sometimes things happen that **interrupt** this schedule, the **schedule must be changed or adjusted**. Answer these questions about Mark's schedule.

1. One day Matt overslept. He woke up at 7:30. How much time did he have to get ready for school that day?

2. One day, Matt's class had a pizza party during their lunch time. They returned to their classroom for the party when the pizzas arrived. The pizzas arrived at 11:30. How did this class's schedule change on that day?

3. One day, students in Mark's class did a special experiment in science class. That day science class did not end until 2:20. How did this affect their schedule?

4. One morning, there was a big storm. The school bus was late; Mark did not get on the bus until 9:00. How do you think this affected the schedule of Mark's class that day?

5. One day the school bus broke down on the way home from school. It was over an hour before it was fixed. Mark arrived home one hour late that day. How do you think his after-school schedule might have been affected?

MY SCHEDULE FOR TODAY

TIME	ACTIVITY

What might happen that would cause your schedule to change?

Leah's soccer team, the Red Team, plays their games during September and October. They must play games with nine other teams and all games must be played by October 31.

All games are scheduled on Fridays or Saturdays. These are the only days that the soccer field can be used. If a game is not played, it must be **rescheduled** for another Friday or Saturday. Look at this soccer schedule. Some games were played, others were not. What could be done to make sure all of the nine games are played by October 31?

OPPONENT	DATE SCHEDULED	RESULT
Blue Team	Sept. 5	won 3 - 1
Purple Team	Sept. 12	rained out
Brown Team	Sept. 18	rained out
White Team	Sept. 19	won 2 - 1
Yellow Team	Sept. 25	rained out
Tan Team	Sept. 26	lost 0 - 3
Orange Team	Oct. 3	won 4 - 2
Green Team	Oct. 17	rained out
Silver Team	Oct. 24	won 4 - 3

These calendar pages show all the days in September and October. How could the coach arrange to make up the games that were rained out and still play all these teams by October 31?

SEPTEMBER						
S	M	T	W	T	F	S
		1	2	3	4	
5	6	7	8	9	10	11
12	13	14	15	16	17	18
19	20	21	22	23	24	25
26	27	28	29	30		

OCTOBER						
S	M	T	W	T	F	S
					1	2
3	4	5	6	7	8	9
10	11	12	13	14	15	16
17	18	19	20	21	22	23
24	25	26	27	28	29	30
31						

Time	Millie	Bus	Ron	Bus	Bob	Bus	Kate	Bus	Gus	Bus	Bonnie	Bus	Dan	Bus	Harry	Bus
6:00 AM	Park St.	A														
6:10 AM	Elm St.	A														
6:20 AM	Maple St.	A														
6:30 AM	Chestnut St.	A	Park St.	B												
6:40 AM	Hillside St.	A	Elm St.	B												
6:50 AM	Mill St.	A	Maple St.	B												
7:00 AM	Zoo	A	Chestnut St.	B	Park St.	C										
7:10 AM	Mill St.	A	Hillside St.	B	Elm St.	C										
7:20 AM	Hillside St.	A	Mill St.	B	Maple St.	C										
7:30 AM	Chestnut St.	A	Zoo	B	Chestnut St.	C	Park St.	D								
7:40 AM	Maple St.	A	Mill St.	B	Hillside St.	C	Elm St.	D								
7:50 AM	Elm St.	A	Hillside St.	B	Mill St.	C	Maple St.	D								
8:00 AM	Park St.	A	Chestnut St.	B	Zoo	C	Chestnut St.	D								
8:10 AM	Elm St.	A	Maple St.	B	Mill St.	C	Hillside St.	D								
8:20 AM	Maple St.	A	Elm St.	B	Hillside St.	C	Mill St.	D								
8:30 AM	Chestnut St.	A	Park St.	B	Chestnut St.	C	Zoo	D								
8:40 AM	Hillside St.	A	Elm St.	B	Maple St.	C	Mill St.	D								
8:50 AM	Mill St.	A	Maple St.	B	Elm St.	C	Hillside St.	D								
9:00 AM	Zoo	A	Chestnut St.	B	Park St.	C	Chestnut St.	D								
9:10 AM	Mill St.	A	Hillside St.	B	Elm St.	C	Maple St.	D								
9:20 AM	Hillside St.	A	Mill St.	B	Maple St.	C	Elm St.	D								
9:30 AM	Chestnut St.	A	Zoo	B	Chestnut St.	C	Park St.	D								
9:40 AM	Maple St.	A	Mill St.	B	Hillside St.	C	Elm St.	D								
9:50 AM	Elm St.	A	Hillside St.	B	Mill St.	C	Maple St.	D								
10:00 AM	Park St.	A	Chestnut St.	B	Zoo	C	Chestnut St.	D	Park St.	A						
10:10 AM	Lunch		Maple St.	B	Mill St.	C	Hillside St.	D	Elm St.	A						
10:20 AM	Lunch		Elm St.	B	Hillside St.	C	Mill St.	D	Maple St.	A						
10:30 AM	Park St.	B	Park St.	B	Chestnut St.	C	Zoo	D	Chestnut St.	A						
10:40 AM	Elm St.	B	Lunch		Maple St.	C	Mill St.	D	Hillside St.	A						
10:50 AM	Maple St.	B	Lunch		Elm St.	C	Hillside St.	D	Mill St.	A						
11:00 AM	Chestnut St.	B	Park St.	C	Park St.	C	Chestnut St.	D	Zoo	A						
11:10 AM	Hillside St.	B	Elm St.	C	Lunch		Maple St.	D	Mill St.	A						
11:20 AM	Mill St.	B	Maple St.	C	Lunch		Elm St.	D	Hillside St.	A						
11:30 AM	Zoo	B	Chestnut St.	C	Park St.	D	Park St.	D	Chestnut St.	A						
11:40 AM	Mill St.	B	Hillside St.	C	Elm St.	D	Lunch		Maple St.	A						
11:50 AM	Hillside St.	B	Mill St.	C	Maple St.	D	Lunch		Elm St.	A						
12:00 PM	Chestnut St.	B	Zoo	C	Chestnut St.	D	Park St.	A	Park St.	A						
12:10 PM	Maple St.	B	Mill St.	C	Hillside St.	D	Elm St.	A								
12:20 PM	Elm St.	B	Hillside St.	C	Mill St.	D	Maple St.	A								
12:30 PM	Park St.	B	Chestnut St.	C	Zoo	D	Chestnut St.	A								
12:40 PM	Elm St.	B	Maple St.	C	Mill St.	D	Hillside St.	A								
12:50 PM	Maple St.	B	Elm St.	C	Hillside St.	D	Mill St.	A								
1:00 PM	Chestnut St.	B	Park St.	C	Chestnut St.	D	Zoo	A								
1:10 PM	Hillside St.	B	Elm St.	C	Maple St.	D	Mill St.	A								
1:20 PM	Mill St.	B	Maple St.	C	Elm St.	D	Hillside St.	A								
1:30 PM	Zoo	B	Chestnut St.	C	Park St.	D	Chestnut St.	A								
1:40 PM	Mill St.	B	Hillside St.	C	Elm St.	D	Maple St.	A								
1:50 PM	Hillside St.	B	Mill St.	C	Maple St.	D	Elm St.	A								
2:00 PM	Chestnut St.	B	Zoo	C	Chestnut St.	D	Park St.	A								
2:10 PM	Maple St.	B	Mill St.	C	Hillside St.	D	Elm St.	A								
2:20 PM	Elm St.	B	Hillside St.	C	Mill St.	D	Maple St.	A								
2:30 PM	Park St.	B	Chestnut St.	C	Zoo	D	Chestnut St.	A	Park St.	B						
2:40 PM			Maple St.	C	Mill St.	D	Hillside St.	A	Elm St.	B						
2:50 PM			Elm St.	C	Hillside St.	D	Mill St.	A	Maple St.	B						
3:00 PM			Park St.	C	Chestnut St.	D	Zoo	A	Chestnut St.	B						
3:10 PM					Maple St.	D	Mill St.	A	Hillside St.	B						
3:20 PM					Elm St.	D	Hillside St.	A	Mill St.	B						
3:30 PM					Park St.	D	Chestnut St.	A	Zoo	B						
3:40 PM							Maple St.	A	Mill St.	B						
3:50 PM							Elm St.	A	Hillside St.	B						
4:00 PM							Park St.	A	Chestnut St.	B						
4:10 PM									Maple St.	B						
4:20 PM									Elm St.	B						
4:30 PM									Park St.	B						
4:40 PM									Elm St.	B						
4:50 PM									Maple St.	B						
5:00 PM									Chestnut St.	B						
5:10 PM									Hillside St.	B	Park St.	C				
5:20 PM									Mill St.	B	Elm St.	C				
5:30 PM									Zoo	B	Maple St.	C				
5:40 PM									Mill St.	B	Chestnut St.	C	Park St.	D		
5:50 PM									Hillside St.	B	Hillside St.	C	Elm St.	D		
6:00 PM									Chestnut St.	B	Mill St.	C	Maple St.	D		
6:10 PM									Maple St.	B	Zoo	C	Chestnut St.	D	Park St.	A
6:20 PM									Elm St.	B	Mill St.	C	Hillside St.	D	Elm St.	A
6:30 PM									Park St.	B	Hillside St.	C	Mill St.	D	Maple St.	A
6:40 PM											Chestnut St.	C	Zoo	D	Chestnut St.	A
6:50 PM											Maple St.	C	Mill St.	D	Hillside St.	A
7:00 PM											Elm St.	C	Hillside St.	D	Mill St.	A
7:10 PM											Park St.	C	Chestnut St.	D	Zoo	A
7:20 PM													Elm St.	D	Mill St.	A
7:30 PM													Maple St.	D	Hillside St.	A

Here are the schedules of eight different drivers who drive the four buses, Bus A, Bus B, Bus C and Bus D from the center to town, Park Street, to the Zoo and back.

Page 78 shows the schedules of the drivers that drive the bus from town to the zoo and back to town. The first bus leaves town at 6:00 in the morning. Millie, Ron, Bob and Kate drive the busses to and from the zoo from the beginnings of their work days to the end. Gus drives their busses when Millie, Ron, Bob and Kate have lunch. He drives Millie's bus from 2:30 in the afternoon, when Millie goes home, until 7:00 in the evening when he goes home. Bonnie, Dan and Harry drive Ron's, Bob's and Kate's busses from the time that each of these drivers goes home until the time when the zoo closes, 6:30. Then they drive different busses until their work day is over. Here are the busses that the drivers drive:

Think about the schedules of these bus drivers as you answer these questions.

1. Who is the first driver to leave town for the zoo in the morning? Who drives the last bus that leaves the zoo for the day? How do you know this?

2. Which bus arrives at the zoo at 10:00? Who is driving? How do you know this?

3. How long does it take one driver to make a complete round trip, leaving Park Street, making all of his stops, then returning to Park Street?

4. Who is the first driver to end the work day?

5. Where do Millie, Ron, Bob and Kate have lunch? How do you know this? What happens to the busses while they're having their lunch?

6. At what time does the driver who goes home at 4:00 have lunch?

7. One driver drives two different busses, has his lunch and works in the garage for two hours. Who is this? (Hint: This driver drives Bus A and Bus B.)

8. Which drivers stop at the zoo at the same time that Millie stops at Chestnut Street? How did you figure this out? (Ron, Kate, Gus)

9. Kate drives the bus that her son, Richard, catches each Wednesday afternoon after school on her way to the zoo. She picks him up in front of his school and drops him off for his guitar lesson at the music studio on Mill Street twenty minutes later. On what street is Richard's school? How do you know this?

10. Name the drivers who drive Bus A, Bus B, Bus C and Bus D. Look at this schedule and discuss reasons why some drivers drive more than one bus during a work day.

Answers on page 105

©Circuit Publications   *Teaching the Language of Time*

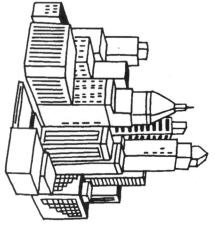

Bus Schedule - Town to Zoo

Location	Bus	A	B	C	D	A	B	C	D	A	B	C	D	A	B	C	D
Depart Town		6:00AM	6:30AM	7:00AM	7:30AM	8:00AM	8:30AM	9:00AM	9:30AM	10:00AM	10:30AM	11:00AM	11:30AM	12:00PM	12:30PM	1:00PM	1:30PM
Elm St.		6:10AM	6:40AM	7:10AM	7:40AM	8:10AM	8:40AM	9:10AM	9:40AM	10:10AM	10:40AM	11:10AM	11:40AM	12:10PM	12:40PM	1:10PM	1:40PM
Maple St.		6:20AM	6:50AM	7:20AM	7:50AM	8:20AM	8:50AM	9:20AM	9:50AM	10:20AM	10:50AM	11:20AM	11:50AM	12:20PM	12:50PM	1:20PM	1:50PM
Chestnut St.		6:30AM	7:00AM	7:30AM	8:00AM	8:30AM	9:00AM	9:30AM	10:00AM	10:30AM	11:00AM	11:30AM	12:00PM	12:30PM	1:00PM	1:30PM	2:00PM
Hillside St.		6:40AM	7:10AM	7:40AM	8:10AM	8:40AM	9:10AM	9:40AM	10:10AM	10:40AM	11:10AM	11:40AM	12:10PM	12:40PM	1:10PM	1:40PM	2:10PM
Mill St.		6:50AM	7:20AM	7:50AM	8:20AM	8:50AM	9:20AM	9:50AM	10:20AM	10:50AM	11:20AM	11:50AM	12:20PM	12:50PM	1:20PM	1:50PM	2:20PM
Arrive Zoo		7:00AM	7:30AM	8:00AM	8:30AM	9:00AM	9:30AM	10:00AM	10:30AM	11:00AM	11:30AM	12:00PM	12:30PM	1:00PM	1:30PM	2:00PM	2:30PM

Location	Bus	A	B	C	D	A	B	C	D
Depart Town		2:00PM	2:30PM	3:00PM	3:30PM	4:00PM	4:30PM	5:00PM	5:30PM
Elm St.		2:10PM	2:40PM	3:10PM	3:40PM	4:10PM	4:40PM	5:10PM	5:40PM
Maple St.		2:20PM	2:50PM	3:20PM	3:50PM	4:20PM	4:50PM	5:20PM	5:50PM
Chestnut St.		2:30PM	3:00PM	3:30PM	4:00PM	4:30PM	5:00PM	5:30PM	6:00PM
Hillside St.		2:40PM	3:10PM	3:40PM	4:10PM	4:40PM	5:10PM	5:40PM	6:10PM
Mill St.		2:50PM	3:20PM	3:50PM	4:20PM	4:50PM	5:20PM	5:50PM	6:20PM
Arrive Zoo		3:00PM	3:30PM	4:00PM	4:30PM	5:00PM	5:30PM	6:00PM	6:30PM

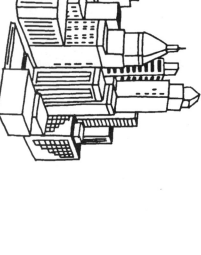

Bus Schedule - Zoo to Town

Location	Bus	A	B	C	D	A	B	C	D	A	B	C	D	A	B	C	D
Depart Zoo		7:00AM	7:30AM	8:00AM	8:30AM	9:00AM	9:30AM	10:00AM	10:30AM	11:00AM	11:30AM	12:00PM	12:30PM	1:00PM	1:30PM	2:00PM	2:30PM
Mill St.		7:10AM	7:40AM	8:10AM	8:40AM	9:10AM	9:40AM	10:10AM	10:40AM	11:10AM	11:40AM	12:10PM	12:40PM	1:10PM	1:40PM	2:10PM	2:40PM
Hillside St.		7:20AM	7:50AM	8:20AM	8:50AM	9:20AM	9:50AM	10:20AM	10:50AM	11:20AM	11:50AM	12:20PM	12:50PM	1:20PM	1:50PM	2:20PM	2:50PM
Chestnut St.		7:30AM	8:00AM	8:30AM	9:00AM	9:30AM	10:00AM	10:30AM	11:00AM	11:30AM	12:00PM	12:30PM	1:00PM	1:30PM	2:00PM	2:30PM	3:00PM
Maple St.		7:40AM	8:10AM	8:40AM	9:10AM	9:40AM	10:10AM	10:40AM	11:10AM	11:40AM	12:10PM	12:40PM	1:10PM	1:40PM	2:10PM	2:40PM	3:10PM
Elm St.		7:50AM	8:20AM	8:50AM	9:20AM	9:50AM	10:20AM	10:50AM	11:20AM	11:50AM	12:20PM	12:50PM	1:20PM	1:50PM	2:20PM	2:50PM	3:20PM
Arrive Town		8:00AM	8:30AM	9:00AM	9:30AM	10:00AM	10:30AM	11:00AM	11:30AM	12:00PM	12:30PM	1:00PM	1:30PM	2:00PM	2:30PM	3:00PM	3:30PM

Location	Bus	A	B	C	D	A	B	C	D
Depart Zoo		3:00PM	3:30PM	4:00PM	4:30PM	5:00PM	5:30PM	6:00PM	6:30PM
Mill St.		3:10PM	3:40PM	4:10PM	4:40PM	5:10PM	5:40PM	6:10PM	6:40PM
Hillside St.		3:20PM	3:50PM	4:20PM	4:50PM	5:20PM	5:50PM	6:20PM	6:50PM
Chestnut St.		3:30PM	4:00PM	4:30PM	5:00PM	5:30PM	6:00PM	6:30PM	7:00PM
Maple St.		3:40PM	4:10PM	4:40PM	5:10PM	5:40PM	6:10PM	6:40PM	7:10PM
Elm St.		3:50PM	4:20PM	4:50PM	5:20PM	5:50PM	6:20PM	6:50PM	7:20PM
Arrive Town		4:00PM	4:30PM	5:00PM	5:30PM	6:00PM	6:30PM	7:00PM	7:30PM

Teaching the Language of Time ©Circuit Publications

Page 80 shows the schedule for the busses that go from the center of town to the zoo. A bus leaves town every ten minutes beginning at 6 o'clock in the morning. The bus stops on Elm Street, Maple Street, Chestnut Street, Hillside Street and Mill Street before it finally reaches the zoo. The last bus leaves the zoo at 6:30 in the evening. Think about each of these people as they ride a bus to the zoo or back.

1. Marcia works taking care of animals at the zoo. She must be at work by 7 o'clock in the morning. She lives on Maple Street. What time must she get on the bus on her street in order to get to work on time? Look at the drivers' schedule on page 78 and find out who the driver of this bus is.

2. Ben works at the zoo. He gets to work by 8 o'clock in the morning and quits at 4 o'clock in the afternoon. He gets on the 4 o'clock bus. What time does he get back to the bus stop on Chestnut Street? Who drives the bus that Ben rides home? (Look on page 78.)

3. Zan and her cousin spent the day at the zoo last Thursday. They got on the last bus leaving the zoo. What time did they get back to the center of town?

4. Sam and his friend left the zoo yesterday on the last bus leaving the zoo. They were going back to the town. The bus broke down on the way back to town and the passengers had to wait for an hour while the bus was fixed. They got back to town an hour later than they were supposed to. What time did they get back? Who was driving this bus? (Look on page 78.)

5. Tony got on the bus in the center of town in the morning and arrived at the zoo after noon. Which bus did he catch in town?

6. The Graysons are planning to meet their friends at the zoo Saturday at 1 o'clock. The bus stops at the end of their street, Maple Street. It takes them 10 minutes to walk from their house to this bus stop. What time must they leave their house in order to meet their friends at the zoo at 1 o'clock as they planned?

7. Last Monday, Roy got on the bus that stops on Elm Street at 10:40 A.M. Peter got on the bus that stops on Hillside Street at 11:10. Who got to the zoo first?

8. Max and Joe spent the day at the zoo last Thursday. They planned to leave the zoo at 4:00, but they decided to stay to see a film about alligators. The film started at 3:45 and lasted an hour. What was the first bus that they could get that would leave the zoo after the film was over?

9. Mr. Hill, the basketball coach at the high school, plans to meet Mr. Jackson, the basketball coach at the junior high, in town after school on Wednesday. The high school is on Mill Street. The school day ends at 3:00. The junior high is on Maple Street. School ends here at 2:30. It's about a 10 minute walk to the bus stops from both schools to the corner of the streets. What would be a good time for the men to plan to meet each other in town?

Answers on page 105

Find words that help you talk about being on time for things that are scheduled for a certain time or period of time. The first letter of each word that you will find is given.

P _____ P _____

O _____ P _____

H _____ O _____

E _____ R _____

E _____ L _____

Q _____ L _____

D _____ P _____

D _____ R _____

A _____ S _____

H _____ T _____

Each of these sentences expresses an idea related to events that occur on a schedule or within certain time periods. Use the words at the bottom of the page to help you fill in these blanks.

1. Steve got a detention for being _____ for school twice last week.

2. You must learn to be _____ when you have a job.

3. The baseball game was _____ for twenty minutes because of rain.

4. If we _____, we might still be able to catch the last train.

5. I had to pay a fine because my library books were _____.

6. Harvey is really _____ when he works in the yard. He can get the lawn mowed and bushes trimmed in less than an hour.

7. Dr. Morrison looked forward to a long _____ vacation when she could relax and get some rest.

8. Our report cards show how many times we were absent or _____.

9. Mr. Brown _____ the meeting that was scheduled for this morning. He will reschedule it for a more convenient time.

10. I try to be _____ for work because my boss gets upset when I'm late.

11. I have an _____ at two o'clock to get my hair cut.

12. Sophie is in trouble because her driver's license is _____.

            expired   tardy   hurry
            appointment   leisurely   delayed
            on time   speedy   punctual
            postponed   overdue   late

©Circuit Publications   Teaching the Language of Time

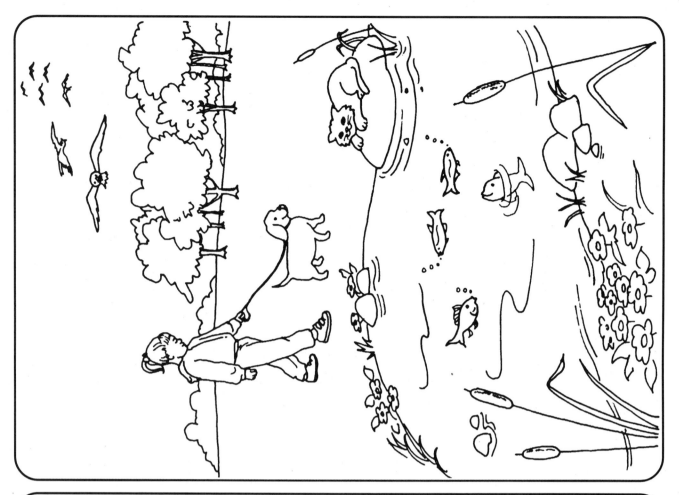

This is how the Earth looks **today**.

This is how the Earth looked **a long time ago**.

Look at the picture of how the world might have looked a long time ago and how it looks today. Answer these questions.

1. What kinds of creatures walked on land a long time ago?

2. What kinds of animals lived in the water a long time ago? What kinds of creatures live in water today?

3. What kinds of creatures flew a long time ago?

4. What kinds of creatures can fly today? What else can we see flying in the sky today?

5. Why don't we see any people in the picture of things a long time ago?

6. Could we travel to a place far away today and see real dinosaurs walking on the land?

7. What does it mean when we say that some animals are extinct?

8. Are there some animals that live today that remind you of animals that are now extinct?

9. What do you think happened to make the Earth change?

10. What do you think our planet might look like millions of years from today?

11. What are some things that could happen on our planet now and in the future that would make it change?

©Circuit Publications　　　Teaching the Language of Time　　　**85**

In the **past** people did many things in different ways than they do things **today**. Think about how people traveled, communicated, farmed and fought in battle in the past. Talk about how these things are done today.

In the past, people used by horse-drawn carriages when they needed to go long distances.

Today, most people drive cars to go long distances.

1. In the past, roads were dirt paths cleared of grass or plants. Some roads were made of bricks or stones. What are roads like today?

2. In the past, people wrote messages to each other by carving pictures in stone. How do people write notes today?

3. In the past, farmers planted seeds by using simple hand tools to prepare the land, plant their seeds and harvest their crops. How do farmers grow our food today?

4. In the past, many people thought that the Earth was flat. What do we know about the shape of our planet today?

5. In the past, people traveled using a horse or small cart pulled by an animal or carried by slaves. Later, people traveled in larger groups on larger vehicles pulled by more than one horse, such as stage coaches. How do large groups of people travel between different cities today?

6. In the past, people were fascinated by birds because they could fly. People wanted to fly just as birds could, but the bodies of people are not designed to fly! Many years ago, a brilliant inventor named Leonardo da Vinci invented the parachute. For many years, people thought that this was the way that people could fly. Talk about how people travel by air today.

7. A long time ago, nations' armies fought in battle riding on horses and wearing armor. People used swords to try to hurt each other and win a battle. How do nations' armies fight today?

In the **past,** people did many things differently than they do **today**. Think about how people took care of themselves and their families in their daily lives.

A long time ago people cooked their meals by placing a pot above a fire.

Today most people use stoves to cook their food.

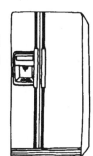

1. In the past, people kept their food cool by storing it under ground where the temperature is a constant cool temperature. What are other ways of keeping food cool? How do we keep food cool today?

2. In the past, people spun yarn from animals' fur or thread from plant fibers. Once the yarn was spun, it could it be knit into sweaters or other warm garments. Thread could be woven into fabric from which shirts and dresses were made. Talk about how your clothes are made today and how this is different from the way it was done a long time ago.

3. A long time ago, when people had something to tell someone who was far away they would communicate their news by using smoke signals. How do people communicate across distances today?

4. In the past, when someone got sick or hurt, he or she went to a wise person in her village who could treat her using medicines made from herbs and plants. Until almost 1900, people did not know that germs caused disease. Talk about how things are different in medicine today. Talk about how some things are the same.

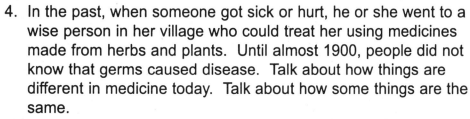

5. In the past, clothes worn by important people were very different from clothes worn by ordinary people. Kings, queens and people of royalty wore crowns and robes made of silk and other special fabrics. Ordinary people wore different types of clothing, usually more simple. How is this different today? What kind of clothing does a president or governor wear when he or she does government jobs? What does she or he wear for fun and relaxation?

6. In the past, and in some places today, not everyone has a chance to learn and grow up to do important things. Not all people born had a chance to decide how the country was governed or who could have special privileges such as education. How is this different today?

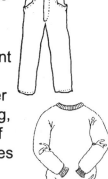
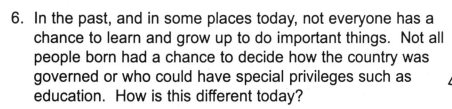

©Circuit Publications — *Teaching the Language of Time*

Find words that help you talk about time and events in the past. Write these words on the lines below. The first letter of each word is given.

[Word search grid]

A ncestor

A ncient

Y esteryear

A ged

P revious

T radition

A ntique

D ated

H istory

B ygone

P rehistoric

P rior

P ast

C entury

E xtinct

S ince

O ld

R emember

O lden

Each of these sentences expresses an idea about something in the past. Use the words at the bottom of the page to help you fill in these blanks.

1. The tyrannosaurus is a _____ animal.

2. His _____ came to this country in the seventeenth century.

3. My cousin wants to study the _____ of Europe because she's interested in things that happened there in the past.

4. Tyrone's uncle is proud of his 1910 Model T Ford. It's a real _____ .

5. We haven't seen Roy for a long time. I don't think we've seen him _____ last summer.

6. The Colonial Period in America is a _____ era.

7. This old lantern is _____ . Electric lights are used now.

8. My grandma _____ what life in this town was like 50 years ago.

9. Carla wants a new coat. Her old coat is out of style and looks _____ .

10. We must work to protect our endangered species so they do not become _____ .

11. Sharon and Bill plan to have a _____ wedding. In many ways their celebration will be the same as their parents' and grandparents' wedding celebrations were.

12. _____ was a special day. There will never be another day exactly like it.

prehistoric	extinct	yesterday
traditional	obsolete	dated
remembers	bygone	history
antique	since	ancestors

Teaching the Language of Time

Find words that help you talk about time and events in the present and future. The first letter of each word is given.

```
F I D F K G H N B V D G T O D A Y H K O J B F V N V E W
U W D F G H J K L P K K Y T D S J L F X S W W R U O I F
T E E T I N G K L J R P K W R L E I N S T A N T Q E V N
U E D N O W B R C U R R E N T R L J B F E W K M W T P C
R Q C B H Y O J B V D Y I P O U Y H G R U B G K L P B E
E D G R L M B Y R C E A W A I T T O U N R E C E N T M V
E R C D H U I L H R H I O P K H G B J I T V D V H M J O
V E X P E C T E R G H M J U J M K O H K K O P L K H F D
Q S F H J I J K O H P Y B G T F O R E S E E O U T F G P
C U L T I M A T E L Y U T G B V L V G K P L M H E W D W
I V F T L Y R F R T U G L L I G V H P R W S W B T U I C
M D B G C O N T E M P O R A R Y N B R W S O C O M I N G
M U N H P O U J E D E Q C T D E P Y G T N J L U N J G E
E V E N T U A L L Y B I I E V M P R E S E N T H R Y J O
D Q H N J K L V F H I L B L H Y U I L P F R D E T Y U L
I R T G H U I F W X D B O Y J J H G D E P R E D I C T I
A Y I Y F V F N V D K I Y J I O P P V D W S F E T T N R
T T G H J T O M O R R O W U Y T P J G V S W F H J L J R
E C Z S D C V T H N U I T B F R W T Q K V B M R Q R T U
F D E T Y Y J Y I O P 0 T G A N T I C I P A T E R J W D
```

F _____ L _____

N _____ T _____

E _____ I _____

U _____ R _____

I _____ F _____

C _____ C _____

E _____ P _____

T _____ P _____

C _____ A _____

A _____

Each of these sentences expresses an idea about something in the present or future. Use the words at the bottom of the page to help you fill in these blanks.

1. I'd like to have a new house with _____ appliances and fixtures.

2. Before the movie began, we saw previews of _____ attractions.

3. She used to be friendly and pleasant, but _____ she's been acting snobbish toward us.

4. My mom didn't have time to brew a pot of coffee so she drank a cup of _____ coffee.

5. If we spend a few hours each week working in the garage we will _____ get it cleaned.

6. The new _____ house being built on our street is very different from most of the others which are older and traditional.

7. Every year, students and teachers anxiously _____ the beginning of summer vacation.

8. I wonder if fortune tellers can really _____ the future when they look into their crystal balls.

9. The manager called the police _____ when she suspected someone was shoplifting.

10. If we don't finish this project today, we'll do it _____ .

11. We _____ him to arrive Tuesday, but he might be delayed a day or two.

12. If the scientists continue to work, they will reach their _____ goal of wiping out this terrible disease.

await	expect	modern
coming	immediately	predict
contemporary	instant	tomorrow
eventually	lately	ultimate

©Circuit Publications   Teaching the Language of Time   91

How far can someone move in a particular amount of time? How fast, or the speed at which something or someone moves, is usually measured in miles per hour (mph). We call this the **rate of speed**. Here are rates of speed at which some animals can move.

cheetah	70 mph	grizzly bear	30 mph
antelope	61 mph	human	28 mph
pigeon	60 mph	elephant	25 mph
horse	48 mph	monarch butterfly	20 mph
elk	45 mph	wild turkey	15 mph
jackrabbit	45 mph	squirrel	12 mph
coyote	43 mph	pig	11 mph
fox	42 mph	chicken	6 mph
zebra	40 mph	spider	1.2 mph
reindeer	32 mph	garden snail	.03 mph
giraffe	32 mph	giant tortoise	.017 mph

Cities and states have laws saying that cars and trucks must not travel at rates of speed beyond safe limits. We see speed limit signs as we drive down streets and highways.

If we see this sign, it means that we may not drive faster than 50 miles per hour.

SPEED LIMIT 50

What do these signs mean?

SPEED LIMIT 25

SPEED LIMIT 35

SPEED LIMIT 65

SPEED LIMIT 20

When people walk, run, ride or drive they travel at different rates of speed. Someone who is walking might be traveling at the rate of four miles per hour (mph). It would take her one hour to walk four miles. Someone running might be traveling at the rate of ten mph. In one hour, she would travel ten miles. The runner would go a longer distance in one hour than the walker because the runner is traveling at a higher or faster rate of speed. Think about the rates of speed at which these people and vehicles travel. Answer these questions.

person walking	2 to 4 mph
person running	6 to 10 mph
person riding a bike	15 mph
car (highway speed)	65 mph
passenger plane	600 mph

Remember, when two people or vehicles are traveling from one point to another, the one traveling at the higher rate of speed will move faster and arrive first.

1. Sal and Mike both plan to travel from Los Angeles to New York City. Sal plans to drive, Mike will travel by plane. Who will arrive in New York first? Why?

2. Wanda and Mike wanted to see who could get from their house to the soccer field which is about ten miles away. Wanda rode her bike, Mike rode a horse. Who do you think got there first? Why?

3. Mr. Kelly just drove from Denver to Colorado Springs. He enjoyed driving his new sports car on the highway where the speed limit was 65 mph. When he got off the highway, he slowed down and drove the rest of the way to his appointment at 35 mph. Why do you think he slowed down if he enjoyed driving at 65 mph?

4. Sara, Alice and Jamie left school at three o'clock for the soccer field which is two miles from school. Alice arrived at the field at 3:15, Sara arrived at 3:20 and Jamie arrived at 3:30. None of the girls rode bikes or went by car. Why do you think they each arrived at a different time?

5. Why do cities and states have speed limits?

6. The speed limit on Plum Street is 35 miles per hour (mph) most of the time. There is a school on Plum Street. The speed limit changes from 35 mph to 20 mph during the times that students are arriving at and leaving school. Why do you think the speed limit goes down during these times?

7. Mr. Clark was driving 45 mph on Furrow Street. The speed limit on Furrow Street is 35 mph. What do you think would happen if a police officer saw Mr. Clark going 45 mph on Furrow Street?

8. Why do you think that people rode horses before cars were invented?

There are many people living in the world today. The longer someone has been alive, the **older** he or she is. These people are different **ages**.

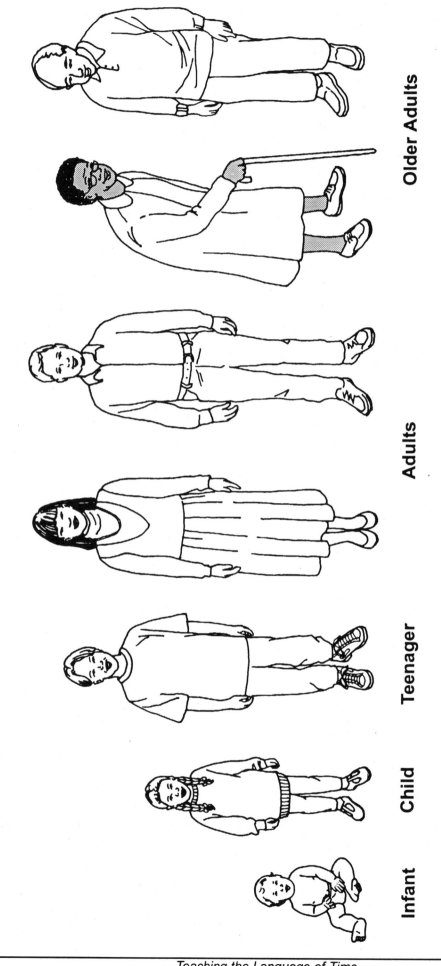

Infant Child Teenager Adults Older Adults

Infant - under 1 year old
Child - from 2 to 12 years old
Teenager - from 13 to 19 years old
Adult - from 20 to 64 years old
Older Adult - over 65 years old

Think about the **ages** of people, how **old** someone is. Answer these questions.

1. How old are you? What is your age?

2. Do you have older or younger brothers or sisters?

3. Who is the oldest person in your family? Who is the youngest?

4. Do you have cousins older or younger than you?

5. Are there any infants in your family or your friends' families?

6. Are there any teenagers in your family or your friends' families?

7. Who are some special adults or grown-ups in your family or among your friends?

8. Are there some older adults or seniors who are special to you?

9. Name three people who are older than you and three people who are younger than you.

---

1. Catherine is 6 months old.
   She is an _____.

2. Carlos is 14 years old.
   He is a _____.

3. Audrey is 75 years old.
   She is an _____.

4. Zoe is 7 years old.
   She is a _____.

5. Max is 42 years old.
   He is an _____.

Think about the ages of the people, animals or things in these exercises. Answer these questions.

1. Cindy is 15 years old, Calvin is 17. Who was born first?

2. Bill is 11 years old, Dan is 13, Ginny is 8 and Flo is 2 years old. Who is the youngest? Who is the oldest? Is anyone older than Flo? Is anyone younger than Flo?

3. There are 5 children in the Wilson family. Penny is 14, Roger is 10, Mark is 8, Yvonne is 19 months and Amanda is 4 months old. How many children are teenagers? Are there infants in this family?

4. When we talk about the order in which children in a family were born, we are talking about the birth order of these children. In the Mason family, Ronald is 3 years old, Gerald is 6, Philip is 2 and Edward is 11. What is the birth order of the children in this family? (Who was born first, second, etc.?)

5. In what year were you born? If someone is 2 years old, in what year was he born? What did you do to figure this out?

6. Rebecca was born in 1988. Sarah was born in 1990. How old is each of the girls today?

7. Richard is 9 years old. He has 5 cousins-Doug who is 15, Roxanne who is 13, Gretchen who is 12, Chet who is 8 and Wendy who is 3. How many of Richard's cousins are older than he is? How many are younger? How do you know this?

8. Cassy's Aunt Lisa will be 30 years old next month. Cassy's mother is 5 years older than Aunt Lisa. Cassy's sister Sheila is 18. Cassy is 10. Who is the youngest? Who is the oldest? Who are adults? Who is a teenager? Who is a child? How old is Aunt Lisa today?

9. Jenny is 7 years old. Her sister Claudia is 5 and her brother Luke is 2. In two years Jenny will be 9. How old will Claudia be when Jenny is 9? How old will Luke be when Claudia is 9? Tell what you did to figure this out.

10. Patrick wants to get a pair of roller blades, but his parents say that he must wait until he is 10 years old. Patrick is only 8. How long will he have to wait before he gets his roller blades? Tell how you figured this out.

11. Nancy has had her bike since she was 11. Nancy's parents said that when her younger sister Jane is 10, Nancy can give her bike to Jane and they will buy Nancy a new bike. Jane is 8. How long will Nancy have to wait for a new bike? How old will Nancy's bike be when she gives it to Jane? Tell how you figured this out.

The girls on Rachel's basketball team were all born in the same year, but some are older or younger than others. That's because each girl was born in a different month! Remember the order of the months of the year:

Months	Rachel's teammates' birthdays
January	Gracie - January 12
February	Toni - March 3
March	Megan - April 24
April	Paula - June 11
May	Rachel - August 27
June	Elizabeth - September 30
July	Stephanie - November 7
August	
September	
October	
November	
December	

The earlier in the year someone is born, the older she is, even though all the girls were born in the same year! Think about why the order of the months is important in these girls' ages.

1. Who is the oldest girl on the basketball team? Who is the youngest? How do you know this?

2. How many girls are older than Paula? How many are younger than she is?

3. When is your birthday? How many years and months old are you?

Remember, there are 12 months in a year. Think about this as you answer these questions.

1. Tammy is 1 year old. Jeremy is 11 months old. Who is older?

2. Eric is 7 years and 2 months old. Bob is 6 years and 11 months old. Who is older? Why?

3. Bonnie had her first birthday 6 months ago. How old is she today? How do you know?

4. Keith's family will have Thanksgiving dinner tomorrow with James and his parents. Keith's eighth birthday was last July. James' eighth birthday was last February. How old will each boy be on Thanksgiving? Who is older?

5. Ryan's birthday is on Christmas Day. He will be 11 on Christmas. Ross will be 11 on New Year's Day. Who is older? Why?

Do you know how many months you have been alive (how many months old you are)? Here's how to find out. There are 12 months in 1 year. For every year you have lived, that is, for every year of your age, you can count 12 months.

On someone's first birthday, she is 12 months old.
On someone's second birthday, he is 24 months old.
On someone's third birthday, he is 36 months old.
On someone's fourth birthday, she is 48 months old.
On someone's fifth birthday, she is 60 months old.
On someone's sixth birthday, he is 72 months old.
On someone's seventh birthday, he is 84 months old.
On someone's eighth birthday, he is 96 months old.
On someone's ninth birthday, she is 108 months old.
On someone's tenth birthday, he is 120 months old.

How old will each of these children be in months on the last day of this year? To find out you must know:

1. **how old someone is (in months) on her birthday**
2. **how many months before her birthday and the end of the year**
3. **the total of these months**

Tell how we know how old each of these children will be in months at the end of the year.

1. Paul will be 7 on January 15.
   On that day, he will be 84 months old.
   There are 11 months between his birthday and the last day of the year.
   How old will Paul be on the last day of the year? What did you do to figure this out?

2. George will be 4 on February 27.
   On his birthday, George will be 48 months old.
   There are 10 months between his birthday and the end of this year.
   How old will George be at the end of the year? What did you do to figure this out?

3. Carla will be 9 on June 30.
   On her birthday, she will be 108 months old.
   There are 6 months between her birthday and the end of this year.
   How old will Carla be on the last day of the year? What did you do to figure this out?

4. Raymond will be 6 on November 25.
   How old will he be in months on his sixth birthday?
   How many months are between his birthday and the end of this year?
   How old will Raymond be on the last day of the year? What did you do to figure this out?

How old will you be in months at the end of this year?
Talk about what you must do to figure this out.

How old would you be if you went to another planet? On Earth you become one year older 365 days from your last birthday. A year is the time it takes a planet to go all the way around the sun. It takes some planets longer to go around the sun than Earth. That's because these are farther away from the sun. It takes some planets less time to go around the sun than the Earth. That's because these are closer to the sun. The closer a planet is to the sun the quicker it goes around the sun. Planets closer to the sun go around the sun in fewer days than planets further from the sun. Here is a list of the planets and the number of days (in Earth time) it takes each one to travel around the sun.

```
Mercury - - - - - - - - 88 Earth days
Venus - - - - - - - - 225 Earth days
Earth - - - - - - - - - 365 Earth days
Mars - - - - - - - - - 687 Earth days
Jupiter - - - - - - - 4333 Earth days
Saturn - - - - - - 10,759 Earth days
Uranus - - - - - 30,685 Earth days
Neptune - - - - 60,190 Earth days
Pluto - - - - - - - 90,800 Earth days
```

1. Mercury goes around the sun in 88 days, much faster than Earth goes around the sun. Is Mercury closer or further from the sun than Earth?

2. Which planet has the most days in its year (that is, which planet takes the most time to go around the sun)?

3. If you are 10 years in Earth days, you are 3650 days old. There are 687 days in a year on Mars. If you went to Mars would you be older or younger in Mars years? How do you know this? (Hint: To calculate age in Mars years, you divide the number of days in one year on Earth by the number of days in one year on Mars, then multiply by the age on Earth.)

4. Is Jupiter closer to the sun or further from the sun than Venus? How can you tell this by looking at the list of planets above?

5. Is Venus closer to the sun or further from the sun than Neptune? How do you know this?

6. If you were born on Pluto and celebrated your birthday at the end of one year on Pluto (90,800 days), how many Earth years old would you be if you then moved to Earth?

7. Three scientists, one from Earth, one from Pluto and one from Jupiter each left their homes on their twentieth birthdays for a meeting on Saturn. They all arrived on Saturn on the same day that they had left their homes. Tell how old in Saturn years each scientist was when he or she arrived?

Answers on page 105

Find words that will help you talk about how old someone is. The first letter of words talking about someone's age is given.

R	Y	J	A	E	U	M	Y	O	U	N	G	X	P	N	I	W	G	R	A	N	D	P	A	R	E	N	T
K	L	T	A	U	W	C	Q	L	Z	G	I	T	K	S	X	T	Y	I	S	F	E	X	K	D	T	H	A
D	I	R	K	V	L	A	N	D	Q	A	J	P	V	A	U	B	E	Z	A	D	U	L	T	P	Q	I	R
S	I	T	M	W	O	V	J	F	A	E	K	E	R	H	V	I	Z	O	D	T	P	M	A	S	U	I	G
A	D	O	L	E	S	C	E	N	T	X	A	E	J	C	I	R	F	L	I	O	X	T	C	E	D	O	I
H	U	L	E	M	R	O	X	Z	I	W	P	R	C	N	U	S	T	P	J	L	Q	V	A	N	E	N	R
F	O	T	X	L	R	P	W	E	Y	N	Z	S	A	O	V	E	I	V	W	L	E	R	V	I	P	O	L
T	I	M	Q	F	K	I	C	U	T	X	L	S	G	R	O	W	N	-	U	P	W	P	B	O	Y	V	M
Y	N	D	I	G	K	Q	A	U	G	L	W	C	H	U	S	I	Z	C	O	M	P	Z	I	R	S	L	G
G	I	M	Q	O	X	T	L	A	I	R	P	B	S	O	P	A	M	A	T	U	R	E	P	C	I	Q	M
X	A	Y	T	E	E	N	A	G	E	O	N	G	J	L	W	F	A	I	K	V	X	T	O	W	F	O	U
H	U	J	L	W	C	G	U	A	L	H	D	V	K	T	S	C	H	I	L	D	O	J	S	Y	W	G	B
D	Y	L	M	D	S	A	I	B	J	N	D	E	V	J	D	Y	K	P	N	F	R	S	M	A	Q	Z	G
P	T	Y	U	H	I	N	F	A	N	T	N	E	L	D	E	R	D	K	D	R	V	Y	A	K	H	A	O
A	F	O	G	D	M	Q	Z	B	P	D	F	J	N	V	Z	O	W	P	B	M	A	I	N	T	S	U	P
R	K	H	D	A	I	V	M	Y	M	S	O	Q	T	O	D	D	L	E	R	D	J	K	D	V	O	S	K
E	A	K	T	B	L	W	B	P	E	L	E	V	L	N	C	S	U	M	Q	G	L	W	O	M	A	N	I
N	S	J	Y	R	V	M	L	R	L	Q	D	A	U	G	K	N	P	D	C	R	B	F	S	A	G	I	V
T	J	L	Q	A	R	F	V	M	U	R	I	S	L	P	F	B	C	Z	U	E	L	J	Q	E	D	F	L
A	G	Y	N	L	D	O	W	O	P	D	E	V	G	K	S	F	A	K	P	G	E	H	K	D	C	E	N

W_____   G_____

O_____   M_____

A_____   C_____

P_____   T_____

Y_____   G_____

T_____   A_____

P_____   S_____

I_____   G_____

B_____   B_____

E_____   M_____

100   *Teaching the Language of Time*   ©Circuit Publications

Each of these sentences talks about ideas of someone's age-how old he or she might be. Use the words at the bottom of the page to help you fill in these blanks.

1. Bonnie likes to take her _____ brother for a ride in his carriage.

2. When someone is over 65 years old, he or she gets a _____ citizen's discount at the theater.

3. My mother always says that some things are the same, but some things are very different between people in her _____ and in mine.

4. My father's father's father is my _____ .

5. Some _____ have their driver's licenses but some people don't drive until they are in their twenties.

6. My cousin is a _____ infant. She is just two days old.

7. Sid acts very _____ for his age. People at work think that he's much older than eighteen.

8. Most people like to have some friends from their own _____ groups-people who are the same ages as they are.

9. When salmon become _____ and are ready to lay eggs, they return to the streams where they were hatched.

10. Most of my aunts and uncles are _____ , somewhere between 40 and 50 years old.

11. Your mother and father are your _____ .

12. Terry is too _____ to get a job. He's only 11 years old. He must wait until he's older.

adults	great grandfather	peer
baby	mature	senior
parents	middle-aged	teenagers
generation	newborn	young

This is Jeff. He is 8 years old. These are some important things that happened during each year of his life.

Age 1 year	Age 2 years	Age 3 years	Age 4 years

Jeff learned to walk and talk.	He got a puppy.	Jeff took his first train ride.	He went to preschool.

Age 5 years	Age 6 years	Age 7 years	Age 8 years

Jeff's family moved to a new house.	He started first grade.	Jeff played on a soccer team.	He went camping for the first time.

As Jeff looks at the years of his life, this is the way he remembers special events that occurred in the order of the years of his life. This is a **timeline** of Jeff's life.

  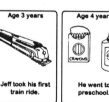 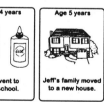  

Use the spaces on the next page to make a timeline of your life, from one point in your life to now. Tell something special about each year of your life in each year since you were in school. Write a sentence, draw a picture or put a photograph in each box. Then line the boxes up in order from the earliest to the latest point. This is a timeline of your life.

Age _____	Age _____
Age _____	Age _____

Teaching the Language of Time

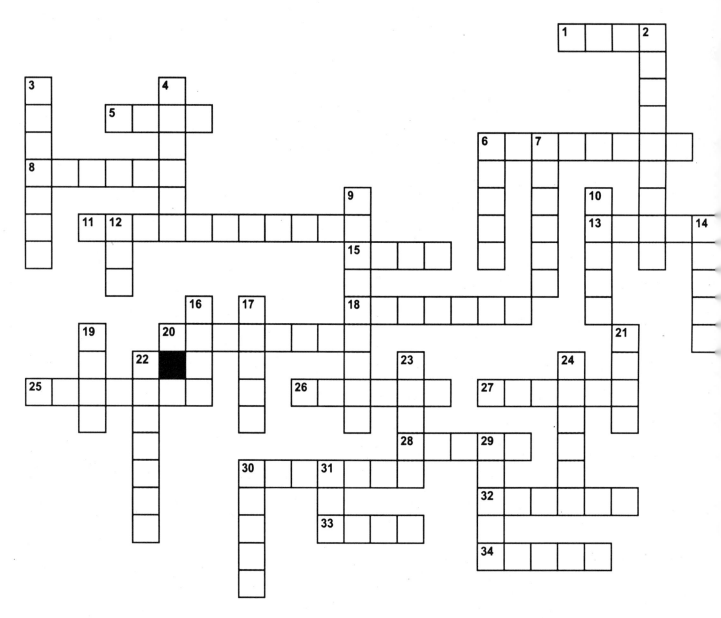

ACROSS
1. time before now
5. 60 minutes
6. day after today
8. 60 of these in one minute
11. 2 things that happen at the same time & place
13. number one
15. in the near future
18. end of a period of time
20. not forget
25. this species no longer lives on this planet
26. spring, summer, autumn, winter
27. not immature
28. not even once
30. time before noon
32. not long ago
33. at which time
34. young one

DOWN
2. not permanent
3. now
4. all of a _____
6. day after yesterday
7. contemporary
9. day before today
10. happens many times
12. not new
14. late
16. following
17. pause
19. month, day, year
21. seven days
22. old and valuable
23. not old
24. after the present
29. before a scheduled time
30. 28 - 31 days
31. present

104 *Teaching the Language of Time* ©Circuit Publications

page 82

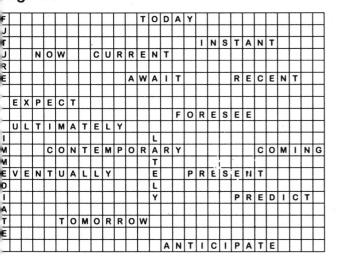

page 88

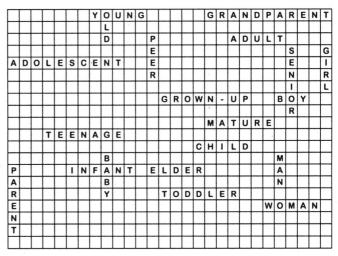

page 90

page 98

page 104

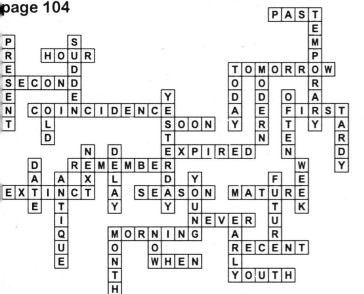

page 79

1. Millie, Dan
2. Bus C, Bob
3. 2 hours
4. Millie
5. Park St.
   Gus drives Bus A
   Millie drives Bus B
   Ron drives Bus C
   Bob drives Bus D
6. Kate, lunch at 11:30
7. Gus
8. Ron, Kate, Gus
9. Chestnut St.
10. Discussion question

page 81

1. 6:20, Millie
2. 4:30, Bonnie
3. 7:30
4. 8:30, Dan
5. Bus D
6. 12:10
7. Both arriced at same time
8. 5:00, Bus D
9. 4:00

page 99

1. closer to
2. Pluto
3. younger
4. further
5. closer to
6. 249 Earth years
7. from Jupiter approx 8 years
   from Earch approx 0.7 years
   from Uranus approx 57 years

Teaching the Language of Time